DREAM BIG
ACT BIG

BREAKTHROUGH AND UNLEASH
THE SUPERSTAR WITHIN YOU

CROIX SATHER

Roger — the superstar —

Dream
Learn more at

Visit us on the web: www.DreamBigActBig.com

© 2011 Croix Sather

Dream Big Act Big. The information presented herein represents the views of the author as of the date of publication. This book is presented for informational purposes only. Due to the rate at which conditions change, the author reserves the right to alter and update his opinions based on new conditions. While every attempt has been made to verify the information in this book, the author does not assume any responsibility for errors, inaccuracies, or omissions.

The author and publisher specifically disclaim any liability, loss, or risk which is incurred as a consequence, directly or indirectly, of the use and application of any of the contents of this work.

Dream Big Act Big may be purchased for educational, business, or sales promotional use. For information, please write: Special Markets Department, Renato Publishing, 36 Tamarack Ave. Suite 267, Danbury, CT 06811 or email at info@dreambigactbig.com

Printed in the United States of America.

Cover design by www.saddlestamp.com
Editing by Thomas Hauck Communications Services
Back cover photo: Jeff Skeirik www.jskyphoto.com

FIRST EDITION

Library of Congress Cataloging-in-Publication Data
Sather, Croix
Dream Big Act Big / Croix Sather. - 1st ed.
p. cm.
ISBN: 978-0-9746178-2-4 Hardcover
ISBN: 978-0-9746178-3-1 Softcover Run Across America Edition

1. Self Improvement   2. Business   3. Education   I. Title.

Croix Sather strongly believes in giving back to the betterment of this small world that we inhabit and the people who share it. Croix Sather supports local, national and international charit[...] Big Act Big books are available in gratitude to organizations that serve at risk adults. [...] www.CroixSather.com

CONTENTS

Stand Tall And Run Boldly Through Life..............................7

Going Down the Wrong Road 10

Secret to Success...13

You Can Make a Living Doing *That*?................................16

Your Breakthrough..21

What Is Success? 28

Life Without Limits...31

What You Focus on Expands 38

You Don't Fit In..43

Friends and Enemies 55

Your Dream is Impossible!...66

Stop Thinking Small! 72

Can You See Your Future? 76

Make the Leap..84

Good Is the Enemy of Great 87

Are You Invisible? 95

Dream The Impossible Dream..98

The Self-Sabotage Cycle...106

Climb Your Mountain 120

Finding Your **ONE** Mountain..124

What All Superstars Do 130

Ten Strategies to Becoming a Superstar.........................132

Becoming the Superstar...152

Epilogue 155

Magic is believing in yourself,
if you can do that, you can make anything happen.
– Johann Wolfgang von Goethe

For my children Macenzie and Remington,
My greatest love.

In appreciation to my TEAM
Crossing the finish line wouldn't be possible without YOU!

Tina, Mom & Dad, Rachel, Ray, Peter and Toki, Dave Wheeler, Heather Hansen O'Neill, Stu Mittleman, Doug Comstock, Marshall Sylver, Erica Sylver, Peg Booth, Jenna Stenderup, Julia Wouk, the Booth team, Alyson Palmer, Dr. Greg Werner, Jon Dupree, Anna Seabrook, Tom Hauck, Don Smith, Jeff Skeirik, Matt Boggs, Michele, Tom, Hanna, and Olivia Ford, Bruce Cornwell, Angela Lussier, Dug McGuirk, AJ Pueden, Jared Michalski, Todd Westphal, Lisa Cory, Dawn Roberts, Tina Miritello, Carmine Coco DeYoung, Jerry Aiyathurai, Kris and Kelly Carter, Tudor Maier, Patty Carnevali, David Goldberg, Elle Febbo, Bruce Goulart, Ira Lee, Michelle Perone, Ray Johnson, Dan Rapley, Carol Kormelink, Gail Vilcu, Doreen Stern, Nild Sansone, Andrew Ness, Janice Brickwood, Andrea Issacs, Michael Gaeta, Cameron Steele, Chris Andrews, Dennis DiPinto, and to ALL my Toastmaster friends, especially WestConn Toastmasters.

In Memory of my brother Darrin
Your love, infectious smile and laughter
will always live on through us.

STAND TALL AND RUN BOLDLY THROUGH LIFE

We can go blindly through life. We can say "poor me" and "why don't I get a break." We can blame the economy, the weather, or our stupid boss. We can play life as a loser or a victim, and blame our circumstances.

Or we can stand tall and run boldly through life – our eyes wide open, a smile so big that we catch mosquitoes in our teeth, a laughter so infectious most will think we lost it – making it an amazing journey and screaming, "This is freakin' awesome!"

We can *Dream Big Act Big*.

Life is a one-shot deal. No do-over, I-wasn't-ready, or best-out-of-three. You get one chance and the game is probably half over.

The best news is that each day is a chance to start fresh. Each day you can begin as if it were a new start. Plus it is never too late to make your life amazing and to leave a legacy, as did many late in life including Granny D, Grandma Moses, and Colonial Harland Sanders.

You've had moments of brilliance and you've had moments of being a superstar. So why is it that you haven't achieved everything you want? You're missing parts of the formula. Most people fall into one of two traps that keep them from their dreams: *fear* or *sabotage*. They are afraid to *act big* – or they act big and then sabotage their success.

There is no medical reason why I'm alive. While riding my bicycle one day I was hit head-on by a drunk driver. By a miracle I survived. What did I do? I let the accident define me in a negative way. I found self-destructive ways to feel important. I went into a cycle of success and sabotage. With each success I would find a way to screw it all up. I made so many mistakes that there was nothing left but to succeed.

It actually goes deeper than fear and sabotage. Pull back the layers of an onion and you get to the core. For most of us we have different versions of the same core. And it is that core that keeps us from the success we want because it is the default self-preservation program. You can let your default programming win and you can survive, or you can take charge of your life and thrive.

Why Is Dream Big Act Big Different?

There is so much more than just the strategies to success in these pages. We also get into the architecture of your mind to uncover your blocks and to program you for success. Yes, there is a formula to success and happiness, but so what? What good is knowing the formula if you don't take action or you take action and then sabotage your successes?

Woven into the fabric of the stories and strategies are the means to uncover and eradicate your self-limiting programs so you can *Break Through and Unleash the Superstar Within You!* You have a choice. This is the most important choice you will ever make in your life. You can believe what others tell you or you can believe that anything is possible and then do it.

Warning

Some of what you read on these pages of this book goes against much of what you have heard and been told. Becoming a superstar is easy if you are willing to do what others won't. Sometimes that means doing the opposite of the herd.

One last thing before we get started. Would you rather have a coach who is honest and truthful and comes from a place of love to help you grow? Or do you want a coach who makes you feel good about your crappy life and give you excuses for the way it is? If you want the first coach, keep reading. If you want to be like the mainstream herd living in mediocrity and be told "its not your fault," then stop right here because you don't get it.

Now let's get started on creating your amazing life.

GOING DOWN THE WRONG ROAD

I couldn't have been more wrong. I signed up for college. College is good, but my decision for a major was terribly off the mark. On my first attempt at college I signed up for a degree program that I had no business being in. None. Absolutely none. Of course I didn't know it at the time, and I didn't have anyone to ask for advice in that stage of my life.

It was the first time that anyone in my family had gone to college.

I grew up in a family that valued earning a living by working in a trade. My father was a carpenter, my brothers worked for my father, my uncle was a carpenter, my grandfather was a painter, and many of my friends dads were in a construction trade. Even my younger sister was a horse handler in her early teens. Not a single person that I was close to had ever been to college. My life was blue collar through and through. I probably wouldn't have asked for advice anyway. After all, at twenty years old, you know everything and your parents and every other adult are idiots.

I graduated high school with a sixty-five average (sixty-five is passing and sixty-four is failing). I am certain that they threw me a few points to get me out of the school. They didn't need another year of my pain-in-the-ass teenage personality roaming the halls and causing grief for the sake of causing grief. During that era of my life it was something that I was particularly good at. Of course right out of school I went to work for my father as a carpenter's apprentice. I had been working with him for a few years during the summer and winter recess breaks. Thing is, I didn't really like it. I stuck with it for a while and became really good, pretty fast. It was exciting because it was new – and yet my heart wasn't truly there.

After two years, I decide that I didn't want to swing a hammer for the rest of my life. I had always known it, but it took two years before I would do something about it. Looking back, I'm happy that it only took two years to start making a change from where I was to where I wanted to be. Many people never take that first step. Being a carpenter is a great life and highly valued. After all, Jesus was a carpenter. But it wasn't for me. It wasn't my passion for a career. The problem was that I didn't know what my passion was. I simply knew that it was not framing houses in sub-zero temperatures.

To this day I still love to build things. I even designed, drafted the plans, and built my current house with my father. As great as this is, and my house is amazing, it is not how I want to make a living day-in and day-out. I get restless. I need more variety. I want to see the world every day and not just two weeks a year when on vacation.

I fought with the idea of doing something other than being a carpenter. While my parents supported me in everything I did, there is something to be said for your sons following in your footsteps and carrying on the family trade. My dad was one of the best craftsmen in the region too. There is also a feeling that cannot be duplicated in any other way than to say, "My father is a craftsman, and I learned everything from him."

Even though it was never spoken, I knew that my parents wanted me to be by my father's side until one day he retired and I would take over the family business. I knew that they also valued making a living with your hands more than any other profession. And that is where my inner conflict began.

I knew that I was different. Just like you know that you are different. That is why you're reading this book. There is a feeling in your gut that you are meant to do something unique to you. You probably have a similar inner conflict because what *you* want to do and what *others* expect you to do are two very different things. You must follow that tempest brewing in your gut and make your dreams real. The answer is already inside you. It's your calling. It is your destiny.

SECRET TO SUCCESS

In this book I will share with you the strategies to success that I have learned, found and developed over the years. Some are learned from the timeless writings of the masters. Gone in the physical sense, they remain eternal in their contribution to the world. Some are from current-day masters I've had the honor of being a student of, and mentored by.

Other lessons are from the school of hard knocks. While the school of hard knocks teaches very valuable lessons, it is a place you want to avoid as much as possible. It is like high school detention – a place where I spent a lot of time. You will learn there, but there are better, faster, happier, and more fun ways to learn than to have a crossed-arm, grumpy teacher looking over your shoulder. I have then synergized and synthesized my experiences with the teachings of the masters to create what you hold in your hands. I am honored to be the conduit of these universal lessons.

Some say that there is a secret to success. They want you to believe that there are hidden formulas and magical elixirs. Bullshit! It is all marketing to sell books and seminars. The reason that some people become superstars and stand out above the rest is because they follow the proven blueprint to success. Certainly you have to stay fresh and contemporary to stand out, and yet the foundation will always be the same. The reason some reach the stars is because that was their target. For those exceptional few there was only one outcome in life – to reach the stars. Follow the same blueprint and you will also be among the stars.

The foundation to become successful is as old as time itself. Anyone can learn it and anyone can become extraordinarily successful. *Anyone!* This may mean fame, wealth, happiness, health, adventure, or love. It often means all of them. Here is the greatest part: once you learn the blueprint for success in one area you can apply it to all areas and truly create a life beyond measure.

So why is extraordinary success so uncommon? That is what you are about to learn. Success leaves clues. In these pages I will uncover those clues for you, the principles, and the blueprint to becoming successful.

Dream Big Act Big is about following your gut feelings. It is about rising above your circumstances and following your dreams. It is about you moving beyond your past and becoming the person you were meant to be. Most importantly this book is about listening to your heart, your gut, and your inner voice that says, "I can do it! One day I will prove what is inside of me and become the person whom I am meant to be!"

I always knew there was a special plan for me. Just like you know that there is something special and unique for you. Reflecting back, I could feel it, just like you can feel it. It is not something you can describe, and yet you know it is there. For many years I denied its existence. Don't make that mistake for too long. After a while you will begin to believe it. Embrace that gift inside you and live up to your potential.

Inside of you is a seed that wants to grow so desperately. Like any plant, if the environment is wrong, it will not grow well, if it ever grows at all. Deprive a plant of water, food, and sun and it remains a seed forever. However, when you nourish that seed with the right food (knowledge), water (action), and sun (faith), that seed grows into a beautiful plant. You are amazing and it is time to blossom.

YOU CAN MAKE A LIVING DOING *THAT*?

I started my journey into higher learning in a two-year community college in Westchester, New York. It was the first of many attempts at earning a college degree. It was the only place that would take a person that squeaked out of high school. I don't remember having any guidance when I started. If I met with a career counselor, he didn't leave an impression or give any great advice.

For inspiration, I looked to the only person whom I admired from an intellectual standpoint. He was my dad's accountant. He drove a better car than us, lived in a nicer neighborhood than us, and he didn't have to freeze his ass off in the brutal New York winters building a house in the snow. He had a job that he could sit at a desk all day and met with clients to chat for an hour, charge them for it, and then have his employees do all the work. At that time this sounded good to me. So I signed up as an accounting major. Even though I was innately good at math, this was one of the dumbest things I have ever tried.

Here is where I made my big mistake. I assumed that a career that is good for someone else would be good for me. I never considered my strengths and certainly never considered my weaknesses. I don't like to get bogged down in details. I don't like sitting still. Plus I had an issue with authority. I still do today. Yeah, I was perfect to become an accountant. As much as I hated being out in the cold, I need to move, so being at a desk all day is not so good. I love to socialize and be around people. Accountants aren't known for their gregarious personalities. And I would have to answer directly to the ultimate authority, Uncle Sam.

Obviously being an accountant was not going to work out for me. It is not the way I'm designed. Too many times we try to fit a square peg into a round hole. Or in my case, put a social butterfly into a cubicle. Have you tried to fit into an environment that you are not designed for? Or worse, just to pay the bills?

If only someone had sat me down and smacked some sense into me. Someone like the Incredible Hulk with a tree trunk to the back of my head. It could have saved more than decade of trial and error before I figured some important things out. If only someone asked me at twenty years old, "What do you *like* to do?" We could have come up to an answer like this.

Croix likes:

Adventure
Variety and
  spontaneity
Talking with people
Being with people
In the spotlight
Thrills and
  challenges
Teaching others
Serving others

Creating
Sharing knowledge
  and experience
Learning and
  growing
Traveling
Making a difference
Being
  entrepreneurial
Dolphins

Croix dislikes:

Authority
Rules for the sake of
  rules
Status quo
Fitting in
Small details
Monotony
Repetition
Cold weather
Bugs

It's your turn. Make your own lists too. It will give you insight into who you are. Go ahead do it now.

I would have wondered how could I make a living with adventure, variety, talking with people, being in the spotlight, and making a difference at the top of my list? If I could do it over, in my twenties I would have been a scuba or skydiving guide, or traveled as a backpacker and studied the cultures of the world.

But at some point you have to start making money. I could have opened a dive shop, or become a travel review expert or a travel and adventure guide to the rich and famous. Those were my dreams that I let fade away. You can't go back, you can only move forward.

While it is fun and sometimes disheartening to think of what could have been, we are where we are because of our experiences and choices. You can let them shape you with regret or you can let them be the foundation for your success. Everything that has happened to me and every choice I have made (good and bad) has happened for a reason, bringing me to where I am today. Embrace your past and move boldly into your future. Dream new dreams and never let them go.

Your favorite activities may be to talk with people. How can you possibly make a living talking with people? Oh, I don't know, maybe you should ask Oprah or Larry King. Ellen Degeneres gets to hang out and laugh with people. Tiger Woods plays golf and gets paid amazing amounts of money. Countless superstars sing for audiences. Many people perform on stage to entertain in Las Vegas or in their own one-person show for children's birthday parties. Some grew up playing in the sandbox making castles and today they are amazing architects. There are even people who get paid to play video games all day. They are testing the new games for problems and weaknesses. Or they get paid tons of money for designing the video games, writing children's stories like the *Harry Potter* series, or by baking cookies like Mrs. Fields. You can even preach the word of God like Joel Osteen and be rewarded handsomely for it.

You can do anything by following your dreams and then finding a way to make money at it. You don't have to be a starving artist to be in a career you love. Starving sucks. And many people do it because they think it is "the price you pay for doing what you love" or because it is more spiritual or honorable to sacrifice. Who sold us that B.S.? That's what poor people say who have given up on their dreams and self-worth. You should be justly rewarded for your talent and your commitment to being extraordinary.

If you haven't made your list of what you like and what you don't like – do it now. Seriously. You wouldn't be reading this book if you didn't want to be successful. So do what a successful person does. This is simple, but not silly. It is important to find out what you are great at and what you would love to do for the next stage of your life.

Keep this list and keep adding to it as new ideas and thoughts come to mind. Under the *like* and *don't like* lists, start creating a list of the things you might love to do. No filtering, this is a creative process at this point.

What I Enjoy & What I Dislike

LIKES	DISLIKES

YOUR BREAKTHROUGH

Bill Gates quits Harvard University to begin a software company in his garage. Michael Jordon is cut from his high school basketball team. Donald Trump builds mega-condos and casinos and finds himself almost a billion dollars upside down in debt. Walt Disney builds an amusement park when everyone said he was crazy. J.K. Rowland, author of the *Harry Potter* series, was living on welfare while writing her first book and is now worth over a billion dollars. Martin Luther King Jr. faced inequality and racial injustice head-on even though he knew he would likely pay with his life. Thomas Edison botched thousands of experiments until he got the result he was after. Babe Ruth held the record for most strikeouts as well as the record for homeruns.

Why and how did these people achieve so much? Why does one overcome immense obstacles while others live in obscurity, mediocrity, or poverty?

The formula for success is simple and yet it is uncommon. If it were common there would be more superstars, more icons, more millionaires, more revolutionary movements, and less poverty, fewer diseases, and less conflict. Most importantly, there would be more love and happiness.

This is a short book with a single purpose. For you to BREAK-THROUGH and UNLEASH the SUPERSTAR within YOU! To make you extraordinary, maybe even the best in the world. To give you the tools, strategies and formula that will allow you to rise above your circumstances and your past to become remarkable.

Being remarkable shouldn't be uncommon. It is possible for everyone to rise to extraordinary and be amazing. Are superstars any smarter than you? Probably not. Are they more savvy than you? That's not it either. Are the better than you? That's definitely not it.

What *is* the difference? What is it that makes someone mega-rich, famous, revolutionary, historical, luminary, or exceptional? My goal is to show you – no, *prove* to you – that anything is possible so you can become an icon in your family, your community, and even in the world.

Dream Big Act Big is a movement to inspire those hungry for more. From coast to coast and all over the world. It is one thing to teach strategies for success. It is another to learn them and then prove that it works. In other words, walk your talk and be the example. Not only am I doing something superhuman to prove that anything is possible, I am also paying it forward. Why would I choose to run 3,000 miles across the country in 100 days? Why would I choose to run over thirty miles each day and give keynote seminar based on this book to audiences living in challenging environments? To prove that you can set you mind on anything and make it come true. *Dream Big* and then *Act Big*. All great accomplishments where started with a dream larger than life. Bigger than what seemed possible and then it happened because of massive, purposeful action.

Are You Insane?

Insanity is getting up and going to work everyday at a job you don't like then coming home too tired to enjoy your family or personal time and then repeating the process for forty years. And then at the end of life you ask, "Is this all there is?"

Too often we get caught up in the mundane day-to-day activities and lose sight of our dreams and plans. We become complacent and accept mediocrity. We take a job we don't like to pay the bills to earn "a decent living." Or we fall victim to the social constructs pressed into us that "it's not possible," "you can't do that," and "it will never work."

The *Dream Big Act Big* run across the country will inspire people to rise up and demand an extraordinary life. Life can be amazing and it can be thrilling. In fact, it must be. To feel alive and feel fulfilled you must grow beyond the restraints of mediocrity and insist that your dreams come true.

I am asked, "Is running 3,000 miles possible? In only 100 days? *And* you're giving a seminar each day?" Yes, it *is* possible. Not only is running 3,000 miles possible, but every day I will be throwing a pebble in the pond, creating waves of hope and inspiration from coast to coast. I am writing this edition of the *Dream Big Act Big* book while I am in training and preparation for the run. During my run from San Diego to New York City I will give a seminar each day to young adults in challenging environments. Plus, at each stop of this inspirational tour, I will be giving away *Dream Big Act Big* books. My goal is to give away 100,000 books. Why? Because I was on the edge of disaster like so many young adults and I wish I would have had a mentor to guide me through the very rough waters of my young life.

Most people want to eliminate a fear. Fear of failure, fear of being lonely, and fear of rejection to name a few. These are good fears to overcome.

There is one fear that I have that I want to keep because this is a healthy fear that propels me forward in life.

This fear is to be at the end of my life and replay my life's movie only to see that I could have done more. To realize that if I only acted instead of letting fear stop me. If I only asked for help when I needed it instead of be ashamed that I couldn't do it alone. If I only stopped accepting "good" and insisted upon "great." My 100-day run is to challenge me and my *100-Day Challenge* is to challenge you to expect and only accept everything great this life has to offer. What can you do in 100 days?

Ultra Success Comes to Those Who Demand it

Ultra success comes to those who decide they *will* succeed and then take massive action to make it happen. When it is unacceptable for anything to happen other than your goal, then and only then, anything is possible. In the words of Susan B. Anthony, women's rights and suffrage leader, "Failure is impossible." It is your responsibility to make big things happen in your life. We are not created to take up space, use oxygen, and add to landfills. We are each born with a gift. The gift is slightly different for every one of us and yet it is the same. It is different because we all have different innate talents and desires. It is the same because each one of has unlimited potential.

Why Are You Here?

There is an unrest inside you because you know there is more to life that you currently have. You have that feeling in your gut that you can achieve more. You have a burning in your heart that tells you that you have a purpose in this life. You have that itch under your skin to know that you will make a difference in the world. It is already inside of you. Nobody gives that to you because you already have it. Inside of you is a seed.

You were born with this seed. It is your seed of greatness. We were designed to be great and nobody can take that away from you – NOBODY! It doesn't matter where you were born, who your parents are, what anyone has done to you, or even the stupid things you have done in your past (yes, we know all about that time when you... well, *you* know!).

There are great dangers in life. There's the danger that you let your dreams and your goals fade away. There's the danger that you do not nourish the seed of greatness within you. There's the danger that you let others convince you to play small and safe. There's the danger that what others think matter more than your thoughts and beliefs. When these happen you will doubt your ability and never reach your potential.

The greatest danger is that you listen and believe the negative chatter inside your mind.

To become the person you are meant to be, to reach your full potential, that seed inside of you must be nourished to grow. You are the guardian of what enters your mind and you are keeper of the thoughts that circulate. Big dreams and an optimistic mindset will get you part-way there. The rest you must learn. So let's get started, Superstar.

Success Is Not Difficult. It's Just Different.

Success is a different way of thinking, a different way of acting, and a different way of behaving. It's different than what most people in the world do. Success is often thought to be an elusive moving target. It can be, when you see it as a final target. True success is not a target at all – success is a mindset and a way of thinking. In the process you will fill your bank account, create amazing relationships, become more spiritual, happy, joyful and fun, and you will live a life of adventure.

If you want the same results as a world-champion athlete, do what he or she does. If you want the same result as a best-selling author, do what he or she does. If you want the same result as the typical person in your neighborhood who is struggling from paycheck to paycheck working at a crappy job with a life filled with ridiculous dramas, do what he or she does.

The formula for success is the same simple formula for failure and the same simple formula for mediocrity.

I'm not speaking in code – here is what I mean. People who are consistent failures have a specific formula to achieve failure. In other words, they have a pattern of behavior that repeats failure. Those who achieve mediocrity have a formula for that result. Success is made out to be this elusive concept obtainable by only the privileged few. But success is simply a formula like any other.

The fact is – you are already successful. You are successful at bringing into your life the things you have. If you are rich or poor, many friends or no friends, happy or depressed, healthy or fat, you have the perfect success formula for achieving the results you are getting.

Many say that I am insane for running across the country. I might be a bit of an adventure junkie, but I am not insane. As the saying goes, insanity is doing the same thing over and over and expecting a different result.

A typical example is John from the fire department where we both volunteered as fire fighters and emergency medical technicians. He would go to work, bitch about his life to buddies, file complaints against others whom he worked with, then do the least effort possible to keep his job. He would come home and complain to his wife, yell at his kids, and want everyone to serve him because he was "the king of the castle." He would come to the firehouse and moan about his job and complain about how his wife and kids drove him up the wall.

John wondered why he was always bypassed for promotions. He would always say, "Why can't I get ahead in life?"

What if you changed the ingredients of your recipe? Would you get a different result? If you bake a cake and your recipe calls for three cups of flour and one cup of sugar but you put in three cups of sugar and one cup of flour, will you get a different result? If you bake a cake and add dirt instead of flour, would you get a very different result? Of course you will. Some people are using dirt in their recipe and expecting a chocolate soufflé from Martha Stewart.

If you want more out of life and the recipe is not working, then change your recipe. If that doesn't work, then change it again, and again, again – until when? Until you get the result you are after. World famous chefs didn't get that way by making a recipe the first time and never improving on it. A great chef will make keep changing the ingredients and methods until he or she gets the result they want. That is why their meals melt in your mouth and have you begging for more.

WHAT IS SUCCESS?

Success is living up to your potential and living your life on your terms. It is up to you to choose the life and create the life that you want. Not anyone else's definition – *yours!* Life is meant to be dreamy and amazing. So great it seems like a fairy tale and you can hardly believe it is true. A life when you wake up in the morning and think, "I am so blessed. This is miraculous." The distinction is that it is a life on your terms and a life that is your fairy tale.

Success is not just wealth and riches. Nor is it just one adventure after another. It isn't even serving your creator or society. These are all parts of it, but none on their own will create an amazing life. It is the abundance of all of these that create an extraordinary life. Success is always moving to a higher standard. It is making a difference in your life and others plus having a fabulous time doing it and getting rewarded well for it.

Some have career and family success but are fat and horrifically unhealthy. Some people have massive wealth and yet they are unhappy and living in emotional turmoil. Others have happiness but have no money and die broke depending on government subsidies and family support. Most go though life as zombies living day-to-day in a gray world, merely surviving. Some get close and become mildly successful and then accept good enough and become complacent.

Some go through life traveling the seven continents. It's one adventure after another. They have lives filled with happiness, love, health and gratitude, plus they make lots of money doing what they love. Sounds pretty cool, huh? This is a rare and an exciting life. This should be and can be yours. Or something even better.

The key to life is our *experiences*. It is our experiences, and those with whom we shared them, that we will remember and cherish. A life without adventure and experiences is a life without meaning. Your experiences give your life meaning. It's not the money that people want, it's the experience that money gives them. It's not the car or the house or the trips, it's the emotions that those things bring to life. Money is just a tool to get there. It's not the spiritual worshiping that people are after, it's the feelings, fulfillment, and faith that it brings.

Years ago I met a man who worked as a doorman in New York City in my client's fancy Upper West Side building. I was early for an appointment, so as I waited in the lobby I chatted it up with the doorman . He was about forty-five or so and had never been anywhere other then about ten blocks from his building. He had never been to Chinatown, the West Side walkway, Coney Island, Statue of Liberty, Empire State Building, or even to the East Side. He was a prisoner without a cage. His prison? His own fears and limiting beliefs.

This is an extreme example, but a very real one. Most people never get close to the things they want because of a fear or old belief system. The doorman's parents had convinced him of how dangerous the world was and that he should never leave their neighborhood. In the

Disney movie *Tangled*, Rapunzel's wicked mother convinces her to stay in the tower because the world is a dangerous place. Rapunzel escapes with the help of Flynn Rider. The doorman was never so fortunate. He will live and die within the radius of a few blocks, never experiencing the world.

Are you the doorman or are you Rapunzel?

If you could have anything in the world and live anyway that you want, how would you live? Would you live where you do? Would you work where you work? Would you be in the same career or field? Who would be your friends?

What would your life be like? Take a few moments right now and write some of the things you would do, be and experience if you could wave a magic wand and make it true.

LIFE WITHOUT LIMITS

Success is about having it all. Success is abundance in health, love, happiness, spirituality, family, friends, fun, excitement, adventure, making contributions, and of course finances. This will mean different things to everyone, and yet it must include all of these. If you are missing any of these for a long period of time, your life will be turbulent and a chore. Notice I didn't define what these words mean. They are symbolic of the important ingredients in life. Your definitions will be different than mine, and that of your friends, family and neighbors. And your definitions will change as you grow and evolve.

The Richest Place in the World

It's easy to think that the richest place on earth is the California coast, with its multimillion-dollar beach homes for hundreds of miles. Or you might think it's in Africa where there are vast deposits of gold and diamonds. You could believe that it's in oil-rich nations of the Middle East, or even in Jerusalem because of it religious history.

On all accounts you would be wrong. Yes, they are all important facts and places, but the richest place on earth is six feet down.

The richest place on earth is the graveyard. Under the countless headstones and in every tomb lies wealth beyond imagine. It is death itself that captures the prosperity of human potential. This is where adventures are never lived, books are never written, inventions never created, stories are never told, art never painted, songs never sung, cures never discovered, love is never shared, where unborn dreams never grow, and where human potential ends.

For some, death comes while still on earth.

Death happens once you stop dreaming and striving for more. It happens when one gives up and moves aimlessly with the crowd and when one lives a life of acceptance and mediocrity.

For others, death never comes. They may leave us in the physical sense but their gifts to the world live on through their accomplishments, the *works* they created and things they did for others while here on earth. Live a life so great that you are never forgotten – like Mark Twain, George Washington, Shakespeare, and Henry Ford.

This is *your* life to create, do, build, find, experience, love, and make anything of it that you choose. There is nobody who can stop you except *you*. Do you want to die with unwritten books, unfulfilled dreams, love never shared, and adventures never experienced? Or are you the one who is going to create it all and be the shining example that inspires others?

How to Be a Loser

Before we can learn on how to be a winner, a champion, and a superstar, let's first define a *loser*. After all, to become a winner you need to do the opposite of what a loser does.

Here are some main strategies to being a world-class loser.

Complain and whine about everything

Blame others

Point your finger at conspiracy

Do only enough to keep your job

Spend more than you make

Quit everything on the first try

Never follow through on your promises

Belittle others

Gossip about others

Be an chronic pessimist

Ambitions? Who needs them?

Get angry and mean easily

Think you are superior to others

Take advantage of others

Lie, cheat, and steal

Abuse people and animals

Mooch off your friends and family

Play Farmville and Mafia Wars in all of your free time and at work

Expect someone else to do it

Sleep until noon

Use the phrase, "It's not my job."

Drink 'til you fall down

Eat 'til you can't get up

Believe lotto is the answer to all of your problems

The Rules of Success (Also My House Rules)

If you are going to be successful and if we are to remain friends, here are some house rules:

No whining

Focus on specific results

Only positive self-talk

Be all about total possibility

Be all about total responsibility

Success starts from the inside

Always make it fun

Live wealthy now

Be the moldable talent

A few more things to keep in mind about success:

It is a marathon, not a sprint race.

The winner always has the most persistence.

Superstars believe in themselves more than what anyone says about them.

Success favors the ones who dream big and rewards the ones who act big!

Success Leaves Clues

Do you want to become a millionaire?
Do what a millionaire does.

Want to become healthy and fit?
Do what a healthy and fit person does.

Want to be happy and fun loving?
Do what happy and fun loving people do.

Want to be broke and miserable?
Do what... you get the point.

We have this crazy social fallacy that being successful is hard and having it together is unusual. We have been programmed to believe that really happy people are delirious or out-of-touch. They might even ask, "What's wrong with her?" As if being happy or giddy is a crime. We are told that being fit is hard work and eating healthy is boring.

It is ridiculous and you have been lied to. You're even lying to yourself.

The media lies to you because drama sells. Your teachers lie to you because they don't actually know it all. Even your parents lie to you because they want to protect you. And you lie to yourself to justify where you are and what you have accomplished. Why are there so many lies? Because it is simpler to make something up or to judge someone else than to model them and ask, "What is she doing to get the result that she is getting?"

Success is as easy as modeling the behavior of people who are successful and stop doing the behaviors that no longer serve you. Failure also leaves clues. If something isn't working for you anymore, stop doing that and do something new.

For example: Want to lose weight? Eat less and exercise more.

Yes, it is essentially that simple. Healthy and fit people eat well and exercise regularly. You don't need a fancy trainer or fitness club membership. You need to get your fat ass off the couch and exercise. Swim, bike, run, speedwalk – anything. You need to push your plate away after you have eaten a reasonable-sized portion. Eating healthy food helps too, but even that isn't necessary for weight loss. If you want to be healthy and fit (which is different than being thin) that's easy too. Eat the right food and mix in some of the important exercises.

Here's the secret. This is really important so read carefully. Are you ready? *Do it every day!* Be consistent. Make it your lifestyle. That's it.

I am being blunt here for a reason. I want you to understand that it is simple. In our sophistication we want things to be hard and complex. If something is hard then we have a way to justify not doing it. Why make it more work than it has to be? Keep it simple and you will succeed. If you are ready for a book that makes fitness simple and easy, get a copy of my book *Better Body Better Life* at Amazon. com and HYPERLINK "http://BetterBodyBetterLife.com"http:// BetterBodyBetterLife.com. Order it from my website and enter the code *dream* and you will get an extra twenty percent off discount.

I get criticized for using the word *fat* instead of overweight. I get it. People want life's challenges to be softened for them with euphemisms and sugar coating.

It's the sugar coating that makes your belly hang over your belt.

Saying, "love handles, a few extra pounds, overweight, big boned, or shapely" does not make you any less unhealthy or fat.

Then the lies start. "Oh, its just a few pounds." A few months later, "I'll start after the new year, its just a little extra weight." When this continues you find yourself ten years down the road and eighty pounds overweight asking, "When the heck did I become a fat bastard?" By the way, that's not a curse, it's a character on *Austin Powers*.

Broke people do the same thing. *Poor* people have little money. *Broke* people are reckless with their money and broke because of their stupid money habits. Broke people spend more than they make and don't save money living beyond their means.

Whatever it is that you want to do better, find someone who does it and do what they do. Better yet, find several people who are achieving what you want to achieve and do those same things that they all do. What are the common traits? Then ask yourself, what do they do differently and what difference is that making in their lives?

For instance, there are many great speakers. While their technical skills may be similar, why is that one speaker will inspire an audience and another doesn't? Is it their words, information, energy level, tone, speed, rhythm, stories – or is it their X-factor? Those small distinctions will sometimes make a massive difference.

If you want to learn how to speak in front of audiences and hone your skills, you don't bring a soapbox into the bar, give a speech, and ask for feedback. That is unless you are behind a cage like in the movie *Roadhouse*. You should go to a Toastmasters meeting to harness the power of public speaking from people who value those skills and have the experience to help you get better.

If you want to have a lifetime of love and passion in your marriage, you might ask loving and passionate couples. You won't invite your cousin who doesn't stay with a woman more than one week or the neighbor who says the secret to a long relationship is a beer, a workshop, and your hearing aide turned off. You also wouldn't ask the couple married fifty years who do nothing but fight and belittle each other. It sounds stupid that you would go and ask a bitter unhappy couple for advice and yet that is what happens when these are the people who raised you and by default you model their behavior because it is the only role models you had for a relationship – or money – or happiness – or health.

When you decide that skydiving has got to be the most intense feeling and fear-crushing activity you can do (and it is), you will *not* go to the top of your house, tie a blanket to your back and jump. You go to people who are experts and can teach you how to *safely* jump out of a perfectly good plane.

Find the true role models and ask them for advice. Most will be thrilled and honored that you asked them.

WHAT YOU FOCUS ON EXPANDS

A friend of mine called me up and asked, "Do you think that my manuscript has enough value, you know, enough validity in it?" I knew what Heather was asking and it had nothing to do with her manuscript. It was jitters at the alter. Her manuscript was finished and she was about to send it to her publisher. It was her first book and she wanted it perfect. In the last moments before she would hit the send button, she doubted herself and her abilities. Heather is a fabulous speaker and writer, and has a special gift to give to the world, but that is not what she was focusing on at the moment.

Heather was focusing on what she didn't have, she was focusing on what she didn't know, and she was focusing and listening to the demons. We all have them in the back of our mind and when you are out of your comfort zone they say, "You're not good enough." Heather was also focusing on her financial challenges instead of her financial opportunities.

I reminded her of how many great authors got started by speaking to audiences and selling their books in advance. I also reminded her about Andy Andrews selling 600,000 copies of his book – and a publisher still wouldn't touch it. And how Jack Canfield and Mark Victor Hansen sold their books out of the trunk of the car as they traveled from small speaking gig to small speaking gig.

To find ways that everyone wins and everyone's life benefits from the relationship, superstars focus on the possibilities and the positives. Heather knew this and simply needed to be reminded. Many people get stuck at this point. They get so close, but then never make the step forward. This happened with my first book. The manuscript sat completed for two years before I had the courage to publish it. By that time I had to go back and update some of the information.

Since Heather is a great speaker she can get out there, speak to audiences and pre-sell her book. To make it very appealing to her audience she can give more value in the form of bonuses for buying a book in advance.

Later that day, Heather hit the send button and her manuscript was off to her publisher. She then shifted gears and started booking speaking events and pre-selling her book. Heather pre-sold her books creating some income from her book before it was printed and her audiences got lots of extra bonuses. Her book, *Find Your Fire at Forty,* is out on the market now.

The Law of Attraction

The law of attraction has been around since people started philosophizing about life. It has been popularized in recent years by a movie and a book. Even though it is in vogue right now, it has been written about for millennia. Most everything in your life is in your life because you attracted it.

You are always sending out waves and pulses of energy. These waves are palpable by others. Ever walk into a room and there was a nasty chill in the room that had nothing to do with the temperature? It because there were two people fighting and you could feel it, you could see it, and you could sense it immediately. Now think to a time where you walked into a room and you could feel the happiness, love and joy. You could sense that too, couldn't you?

You are always sending out energy. It is different depending on the mood you are in and where your state of mind happens to be at any given moment. It is not moment-to-moment energy; we all have off-moments when we are not like ourselves. The law of attraction works on the *overall* energy you send out. What energy are you sending out the majority of the time? If you focus on the negative, more negative and bad events will occur in your life. If you focus on the positive and greatness in your life, more greatness will enter your life.

This affects for more than just things; it affects events, people, and experiences. People are attracted to people who are like them and it goes way beyond the obvious of having similar passions and preferences. People who like to commiserate and complain hang out with others who do the same. People who are athletic have friends who are also athletic. These are activities that attract people to each other. People are attracted to others because they have the same energy. Sometimes you can't explain it. You might even say, "I don't know what it is about him, but there is something I really like."

Remember a time that you were massively attracted to another person. It was visceral. You didn't need to speak a word because there was "chemistry." It is the unspoken, yet completely real attraction of energy, subconscious psychology, physiology, and even biology.

A person who spends most of their time in a positive space focusing on the great will attract more great people, events and things into his or her life. Have you ever met someone who always seems to have amazing luck? Wins the raffles, meets amazing people, has an endless list of clients, and is offered fabulous gifts or invited to incredible parties? That is because they expect that to happen and they attract it into their life. Like energy is attracted to like energy.

Does this mean that the only thing I have to do is expect great things to come into my life and it will happen? Yes and no. You must come from a place of gratitude and truly be in a positive place and be thrilled with whatever comes your way. And if something doesn't, "Hey, that's cool! Something else will appear in my life later."

You bump into someone at the supermarket and she starts to talk to like you are old friends. You know that you know her name, but at that moment your mind is blank. You try hard to remember her name, but the more you try, the more it's blocked. You continue the conversation politely and then head home. Then five minutes later when you are in your car driving, it pops into your head. Great, that doesn't help you now. You say to yourself, "Why couldn't I remember that in the store?"

You don't remember when you are talking to her because you are *forcing* it. Try to force something great into your life and it will evade you.

Graciously accept everything in your life – the good, great and everything else – expect more great things to come into your life, set your intentions on what you desire, and amazing things will happen for you all the time. Be happy in the moment and if you are not, find something to be happy about and shift to that happy energy. Help more amazing things come into your life by anticipating them and asking for them. Not demanding them. Say it out loud, "I am blessed, I am positive, I am a gift to others. Amazing people, events and things enter my life everyday. I deserve all of the great things this life has to offer."

Does this mean that you will never have unfortunate or challenging events happen in your life? No, of course not. As Forrest Gump so intelligently said, "*It* happens" to everyone. Be grateful, even when things aren't going your way. They could be better and they could be worse, and often they turn out to be blessings in disguise.

One thing is certainly true about the law of attraction: It is only part of the formula. You can try to manifest things into your life all day long, but if you are not taking inspired and purposeful action, you are not going to get what you want. The law of attraction is very important and it works, but not without you.

"Do not ask the Lord to guide your footsteps, if you are not willing to move your feet." – Unknown

YOU DON'T FIT IN

Some people are different. Some people don't fit in. They stand out. Never quite meshing into any clique. They are rebels, nonconformists, outliers, trendsetters, and consistent failures. In other words they are superstars. People like Steve Jobs, Muhammad Ali, Richard Branson, Jack Lalanne, Louise Hay, and Sumner Redstone.

You are one of those people – someone who hears a different orchestra. You have ideas that are strange and you think outside the box. Sometimes you are uncomfortable sharing your ideas with others because of how they typically respond. You are a trendsetter and an outlier. One of my clients described it as, "I have always felt like an alien from another planet." What she once perceived as shortcomings are now her assets. She is a rising superstar now speaking on world-famous stages.

It is a blessing that you are not normal. Normal is average, typical and bland. You never see a picture of Bob on the cover of *Time* magazine with the byline *What It's Like to Be Normal*. Why would anyone want to be normal, when normal means being like millions of others? It means working in a cubicle at a job that doesn't even pay the bills for forty hours a week and with only two weeks vacation. Reminds you of the Apple Macintosh commercial 1984, doesn't it? Normal happens to good people and even great people when they are seduced into the social norms of keeping up with the Joneses. Don't keep up with the Joneses. Be the one that the Jones family emulates.

If you have this strange and unexplainable feeling that you just don't fit in, you are blessed. If you have a feeling of unrest, you should be happy. If you have a pang of dissatisfaction, you should get excited. Embrace those feelings knowing that the superstar within you wants to get out. Give your inner superstar permission to be different, to be bold, to be amazing. Embrace your uniqueness. Give yourself permission to follow your gut feeling, act on your ideas, and go after your dream.

Run bravely towards your purpose and your calling.

I knew I was a different kind of kid when I didn't fit in to any clique. I certainly wasn't a jock and I didn't follow sports much. The popular and pretty people snubbed me. I wasn't in the same hemisphere as the intellectuals. I wasn't an artist or a geek. I didn't even fit in with the troublemakers! For most of my childhood I floated around the outside of many groups with the exception of a few friends who have lasted for many seasons of my life.

Back then, I didn't realize that it was a good thing to be apart from the herd and to be the outlier. The challenge was that I didn't know that this meant I should be forging my own path and focusing my energy on creating, learning, and doing. Instead I let my energetic and rambunctious ideas get me in trouble.

I have always lived a bit on the edge. Even as a preteen I was looking for the adventure in life. Pushing the boundaries and standing out for my fearless exuberance. (Mom and dad, you may not want to read the rest of this paragraph. This will be news to you.) I would jumping off the roof of my friend's house. Not because he dared me to, only because I thought it would be fun. With the help of that same friend we tied a rope to a big tree and then tied it to the post of my bicycle. I would then ride as fast as I could until the rope became taught, raising my back tire off the ground catapulting me ten or fifteen feet. I never could figure out why I was the only one doing this stuff. We would dig out snow forts from plowed snow piles and throw snowballs at people and cars passing by. Mostly this was mostly childish behavior with no harm and no foul.

Looking back at your life you may remember that you were different and you didn't fit in like others did. Most of the greatest movers and shakers didn't fit in either. Instead they embraced it . What if Robin Williams, Whoopi Goldberg, Ellen Degeneres, Walt Disney, the Incredible Hulk Lou Ferrigno, or Indra K. Nooyi of Pepsi made an effort to fit in and be normal? They have given the world amazing contributions for embracing their unique talents.

What is the world missing out on because you are playing it safe and trying to fit in?

Life Changes In a Moment

My friends and I had just left the mall on our bicycles. We were fourteen and in those days malls were a novelty. As we were riding home, I was on the right side of the road riding with traffic and my friends were riding on the shoulder on the left riding into traffic. As we rode up towards the crest of the road a drunk driver came speeding over the hill. She saw my friends and swerved to miss them. She did. I imagine that she was looking back thinking out loud, "Oh my God that was close." She never saw me. She didn't swerve away, slow down or jam on the breaks. Her speeding car hit me head on at full speed.

My bike was crushed under the metal bumper of her car. I was launched up and over the hood, ricocheting off the windshield and into the air. According to the police report, I flew fifty feet before my mangled body came crashing back down to the pavement.

My parent's best friends were emergency medical technicians and lived just one block away. They arrived on the scene within moments unaware of whom they were coming to help.

My injuries were so extensive that I was rushed thirty miles south to a trauma center. When my parents arrived they didn't recognize the bloody mess of a boy they were looking at. It was the kind of image that inspires horror movies. The neurosurgeon came out of the trauma room. He looked at my parents and said, "I am sorry. We have done everything that we can. If your son survives the night, he will be a vegetable for the rest of his life."

I now have two little children and I cannot imagine being on the receiving end of that conversation. To this day my parents shutter in the memories of that day. I was in a coma for almost four days. I remember three brief moments of those days. When I was in the intensive care unit (ICU) I remember waking up and I was alone. I looked around and somehow understood where I was. I looked down at my bare chest and saw the wires and tubes all over me. I tried to call out to a nurse, but it didn't work. So I did what was true to nature. I found a way to get attention. I pulled all of the leads off my chest and the heart monitor went flatline. Bzzzzzzzzzzz.

An army of nurses and doctors came running in. I remember a tall, very thin, dark-receding-haired doctor coming in calmly behind the nurses. I raised my head, looked up to him and asked, "Can I have some juice?" The doc rolled his eyes and before he could turn around to leave I was passed out again.

A couple of days later I remember waking up and being rolled onto my side. Wondering why I was in this position I looked over my shoulder and there was a beautiful blonde nurse giving me a sponge bath. For a fourteen-year-old this was a very cool deal. The accident did have its benefits. I must have fallen back into unconsciousness. When I woke up again I looked back over my shoulder and it was not the beautiful young nurse giving me a sponge bath but someone who looked like Mimi from the Drew Carey show. Obviously what felt like a moment was really a day later. I was very disappointed.

The third thing I remember was waking up to full awareness. It was almost four days later on a sunny Monday afternoon. The first thing I saw was my mother, and standing behind her was my dad. They never left my side. For the next two weeks in the hospital at least one of them were always there by my side. And they have never left me since. I am blessed. I have had both parents there as my ballast when I need help keeping my ship afloat.

Before the accident I was a spectacular swimmer. I raced five age groups higher and would always place in the top three in freestyle. I am certain that I am a mutant with gills behind my ears. Swimming was the only sport that I truly loved. But after the accident I lost my drive. I never went back to competitive swimming. And because of that, I lost my only identity in which I was a success.

So I found other ways to find significance, but now I found it in unfocused and self-destructive ways.

We have so much energy and emotion tied to our identity. When we lose our identity or it is threatened by change, it can dramatically affect our emotional stability and well-being. Your identity may be as a mom, dad, spouse, coach, accountant, pilot, or marathon runner. Often we have multiple identities because we lead dynamic lives. Most often we identify with one core identity. For men it is typically what they do for a living such as lawyer, plumber, or teacher. For women it is often more complicated. A professional working woman may struggle with her core identity because she is doctor and she is also a mom. Both compete for the primary position. Intellectually she may identify with her profession, but biologically and emotionally she may identify with the role of mom. So she is always struggling to keep the balance between June Cleaver and Meg Whitman.

Career as Identity

Mark spent the better part of thirty years working for a Fortune 100 company. He was passionate about what he did as a patent attorney. He would introduce himself to others as an attorney and was very proud of his work.

In the late 1980s big corporation pink slips were handed out in the thousands. Mark missed the first two rounds. On the third round he was offered a forced early retirement. He was devastated. "How can they do this to me? I've been with them faithfully for twenty-seven years. I am only fifty-four. And I'm one of their top attorneys. How can they do this and take half my pension?" he would moan. Mark became depressed because he no longer had a purpose and he no longer could identify with his profession. For over a year he tried to find a new job. Then he decided to take matters into his own hands and he started his own private practice specializing in patents. Mark was tied to his identity through and through.

My accident occurred on the last day of school before summer break. I was in plaster casts on my arm and leg all summer, and missed the swimming season. By the time the next summer rolled around, I no longer cared much about swimming. I joined the team again for one season, but then quit. From then on I started finding other things to occupy my time. With my flair for adventure, the road I headed down was a dangerous one. I began to pick fights. This was a challenge because I was the smallest student out of three hundred classmates and my opponents were always the largest guys I could find. Strangely enough I held my own against others who were twice my size. Then I picked a fight with a guy one year older but similar to my size. I thought to myself, "This will be easy."

Billy was a human hurricane. For the next five minutes he tossed me around like a rag doll.

Looking back now, I can clearly see that the opponents that seem formidable are often easy to overcome. The small, seemingly easy challenges are the ones that keep knocking you down.

I was reminded about this law of life when I was in college. This was my second round at trying to succeed in college. I needed a physical education course to complete my degree. I remembered watching the boxing matches of Muhammad Ali with my dad when I was a child, and of course the movie *Rocky*. I signed up for boxing. In my early twenties, it seemed like a great way to vent my frustrations on some other guy's face.

After weeks of learning fundamentals it was time to spar. I aggressively stepped forward to go first. The coach must have seen where my head was and he paired me with a seasoned boxer who was my size. We started slow and then I wanted to open up the pain on him. I got two full-force swings on him. He gracefully moved out of the way of the first one. The second one made full contact. He shook it off, looked at the coach, and the coach nodded back in confirmation. It was the same nod of approval that Mr. Miyagi gives the Karate kid. Then my opponent let me have it. After about thirty seconds I felt like I had gone fifteen rounds with Mike Tyson.

You never know who or what is going to toss you a beating. So many times we make something small into a huge fear, blowing it way out of proportion, only to find out later that it was no big deal. Sometimes we are overconfident or ignore the small challenges, thinking they are no big deal – and they are the ones that keep us from growing and getting what we want.

A real life example is when you have a track playing and replaying in your head. Even though it was an event that happened days ago or sometimes decades ago, you continue to replay the scene in your head over and over just like that time you got off the "It's a Small World After All" ride at Disneyland. The more it plays in your head the worse it seems or the worse it makes you feel. If this goes unaltered it can spiral you down in to aggression or depression. It's often the little things that can have a massive impact. If someone has a bad experience in the water as a child, he or she may never learn to swim. If you're selling to someone and they suddenly go ballistic on you, selling will make you uncomfortable, even though that person was having a really bad day and it had nothing to do with you.

If you did something that you wish you had not, it can wreck havoc on your psyche.

It's these mental car crashes that derail us. If you let them go unaltered, these small events will form new beliefs and shape the rest of your life. This is especially true in relationships and most importantly in your relationship with yourself.

Getting Beyond Mental Car Crashes

The most effective way is to reframe the event and then take action to overcome your fear. If it's swimming, alter the story in your mind, saying something like, "My older brother was trying to be funny when he dunked me under the water and I now know that it was just an immature thing to do. I know that millions of people learn to swim and I can too." And then, to conquer your, fear go take swimming lessons with a great coach. In the selling event, reframe it as someone went ballistic on you. That person could have just got news that his wife left him, a family member died, or he lost his job. The way someone reacts has nothing to do with you and everything to do with them and the currents happening in their life.

I could have spent my life angry with the drunk driver who hit me on my bicycle. What good would that do? Instead I have learned to empathize. To be drunk in the early afternoon, she needs help with her addiction. And it must have be horrific for her to see a little boy fly into her windshield, shattering it, and then lie lifeless on the ground as she waited for the ambulance and the police. I never saw her again. I hope that the car accident scared her into AA. I like to believe that she is now an advocate for sobriety and helps other addicts. I'll never know, but that is the reframe I will always believe. One thing I do know without a doubt, is that the car accident radically altered my life. At first it was seemed so random and cruel. "Why would this happen to me?" It sent me into a downward spiral for years. Many years later it became clear why this would happen and how it has positively shaped my life.

Love The One You're With

In 1970 Stephen Stills released "Love the One You're With" as a single and it quickly rose to number fourteen on the Billboard Top 40. The song says to *love the one you're with,* meaning the one next to you. The song got it wrong. First you must love the one you are always with. The most important person in the world – *you.*

What does loving yourself have to do with becoming a superstar? Everything. If you do not love yourself, if you do not believe in yourself, if you do not value yourself, how will anyone else? Why would someone want to help you, support you, admire you, and love you if you do not love yourself? To help others and be of value to others as a superstar, you have got to start from within by loving yourself and being your own greatest fan.

Tiny Pegs and Great Buildings

One of the more beautiful ways of building a house is with a method called *timber framing.* It has a distinctive style that you recognize immediately. Often majestic timber-framed buildings are used for ski lodges and expensive homes in the mountains. Japanese buildings have been using this type of construction for well over one thousand years. In this type of construction massive wooden beams are used as the structure. They are left exposed to admire the size, beauty, and craftsmanship. To join these tremendous beams a joint called mortise and tendon allows the wooden members to fit together like the piece of a puzzle. The detail and work is truly amazing. It is not the just the joint that holds the building together – its strength depends on the a little piece called a *peg*. In the largest most majestic buildings these pegs are tiny in comparison at only three inches round by ten inches long. The timbers fit together in the mortise and tendon cutout (think of the game Jenga) and then a hole the size of the peg is drilled through both timbers at the overlap of the joint. Then the peg is hammered flush and the joint is complete. Without the peg there is no strength in the building.

The pegs are those little things in life that matter as much as the timbers themselves. Loving yourself and believing in yourself as having unlimited potential are some of those "little things' that we often ignore because it seems silly or vain. You were probably not taught this crucial lesson and so you must learn how to have unstoppable and unyielding belief in yourself. If you do not love and value yourself you will always be looking for someone else's approval. You will always need validation from others.

Wanting validation is human, but *needing* validation is weakness. Strength comes from within and it is something that needs to be developed and nourished. You probably had parents who told you, "Don't brag" or "Don't be a show off." They were trying to raise a polite child, and that was really bad advice. In trying to raise a well-behaved and courteous little person they ended up sabotaging your self-confidence. When you do something great you must be your own biggest fan and be proud of yourself. Validate yourself instead of looking to others to validate you. Do you think that Tiger Woods's father ever told him, "Son, you know better than to show off. Let the other kids win." Be the best you can be so that you inspire others to do better. It is not cool to be arrogant. It is very cool to be confident and bold.

In many of my hypnotherapy clients I find that nobody gave the client permission to be amazing. Nobody told them that they should give themselves permission to be superstar. When my client lets go of the old limiting belief (instilled by a well-meaning authority figure like a parent or teacher) to play down their accomplishments and adopts the new belief to be self-congratulatory and frequently self-praising, their life always becomes massively better.

How often do you say to yourself, "Dumbass," "I can't believe I am so stupid," or "I hate myself"? Most people do when they're frustrated or just did something they wish they hadn't. When you say this to yourself you are programming yourself for more mistakes and lowering your confidence. When you catch yourself saying something like these negative phrases to yourself, either out loud or in your mind, immediately stop in the moment. Rephrase what you just said in a way that is encouraging and helpful. Instead of "Dumbass," say, "That was an interesting thing *to do,* and it was also a great effort. Next time I will do [*insert idea*] instead."

Immediately do something to remedy the situation. We all make and do things that we wished we didn't. Even when I am on stage in front of hundreds of people, if I slip with the phrasing of an archaic phrase or belief, I will say to the audience, "Wait, that is not what I meant. That is old programming. I meant to say this…." It is that important. If we aren't making mistakes, we aren't living an exciting, fun, and adventurous life.

Be bold, make mistakes, correct them when necessary, and move on.

How do you develop an "I am a superstar" level of confidence and believing in yourself? Act like a child who just scored the winning point or like you just found out that you won a million dollars. Jump up and down and scream, "I rock!" after any accomplishment. Most people won't do this. And most people will never win a million dollars. Superstars do things differently. When I accomplish something amazing I will stand up and do a (really bad) dance and shout, "Yeah baby! I freakin' rock!" It doesn't matter where I am. This may seem odd to "normal" people. And that is exactly why you must do it. You program your inner mind for success and you build the muscle of unyielding confidence.

You are amazing and a one-of-a-kind gift to this world. You are special and unique in a way that only you can be. You deserve all of the great things that life has to offer. You deserve to be happy, healthy, loved, and prosperous. You are the only one who has your experiences, education, dreams, beliefs, and hopes. Like a fingerprint, you are an original and like a Picasso, a masterpiece. You also have talents and value to give to others that will enrich their lives that can make you financially wealthy.

Give yourself permission to shine, to succeed, to be different, to be a leader, to be an expert, to be fabulous person, and to be a superstar. Believe in yourself as if you are the chosen one because you are.

FRIENDS AND ENEMIES

When you were young, your parents worried about who your friends were. You've heard it hundreds of times, "I don't care what your friends wear, you are not going out of the house looking like that." So you layer "approved" clothes over your cool clothes to leave the house only to be removed once you are out of sight so you can be like your friends. You also heard, "I don't care what Johnny does, you are not going to that party." And probably many more global protective phrases.

Every good parent worries about their child's friends. Why? Because children will turn out to be just like those other children they hang out with. They will dress the same, talk the same, do the same things, and like most of the same things. It starts as young as three or four and grows stronger into tweens, then teens, and the college. When does this stop being a factor? Your twenties, thirties, forties? It never does. It is *always* a factor in your life.

It is commonly said that you are the average of the five people you are around the most. This is wrong! You are the average of the five people who have influenced you the most. Your circle of friends and family will represent those values. A person who is negative and pessimistic will only keep company with other people he or she can commiserate with or people insecure enough to deal with the whining. A sports fanatic will spend most of his time with others who are as crazy about the same sports as he is. Book clubs, civic groups, political affiliations, and raw food niches thrive because of our need to be with others who are like us. You won't join a scuba club to find people who like to knit. Like attracts like, unless you make a purposeful decision to rise to the next level.

Toxic People Will Kill Your Dreams

It is argued that every human has cancer. The gene is in you and surfaces in part by your genetics and in part by your lifestyle or environment. I'm not a doctor or a scientist, but I am certain about this. We all have an emotional cancer than can stay dormant forever or it can be manifested into reality if we let it or let others do it for us. Negative people will kill your dreams and mutate into an emotional cancer in you of self-doubt and self-loathing.

Toxic people include the obvious co-worker who belittles you and tears you down on a daily basis. They are your friends who challenge your ideas and dismiss them as frivolous or dumb. They are the people who roll their eyes at your ideas and the people who ask, "Why are you always working so hard?"

The most unexpected sabotage comes from the people whom you expect to support you and love you and want the best for you. Your parents, siblings, relatives, teachers, and closest friends. The problem is that they *DO* love you and they want to protect you by *THEIR* belief and value system. Those closest in your life want to see you safe and keep you from disappointment and failure.

The quickest way to failure is to live your life down to someone else's rules and values.

A father who believes that hard work, a good education, and a corporate job is the only legitimate way to an honorable life will discourage you from your entrepreneurial spirit and from opening a small business. This is illustrated perfectly in Robert Kiyosaki's book *Rich Dad, Poor Dad*.

Friends who are corporate to the core will not understand why you would want to risk your time and money on a business venture. They won't understand that you want to create something and that you want more out of life than paying your mortgage and painting your picket fence. They will champion for you to stay with the Fortune 500 company and play it safe even though none of them really like their work and they live for their annual pilgrimage to the shore for a two-week vacation. "You got it made here. Put more money in your 401k and buy mutual funds. In a few years you'll be up to three weeks vacation," they say.

Go to the ocean and fish out some crabs. Put them in a large bucket without a lid and watch society in action. An entrepreneurial crab will climb out of the pile, step to the edge, reach for the rim and start to climb out. The other crabs are looking at him and watching in awe. Then one of those crabs thinks, "Hey wait, where are you going?" He grabs the leg of the one that is about to climb out and pulls him back in. The crab tries again and is pulled back in. Other crabs try to climb out and the others pull them back in. A crab will rarely get his freedom because of the other crabs he is living with.

Moral of the story – don't get caught with crabs.

Society is the same. When you go after something better than what the others have, those around you will pull you back down to their level. It may be vindictive and may be done out of protection or love. This happens because when you attain more, when you reach your goals, those close to you have to look at themselves and evaluate why *they* are not getting what *they* want. Instead of growing with you, instead of being inspired to want more and get more, they want to keep you at their level.

One of my coaching clients called me one day and was venting about how she felt "guilty." I asked why? Michelle told me about her vacation with her family. Her mom, dad, brothers and sisters and their families all go on vacation together each year. They rent a huge house and live together for a week. Shivers went down my spine as she filled in the details of how her mom beat her down about "finding a husband." Her dad groaned about her needing a "real job." He said, "Stop that health consulting foolishness. Nobody needs advice on how to eat. You put food on your plate and then in your mouth. What else is there to know?" Michelle kept it together, but by the end of the week she wanted to scream.

I told Michelle, "Fire your family."
"I can't do that. They are my family," she rebutted.

"Michelle, I don't mean literally disown them," I said. "Just limit how much time you spend with them. They obviously love you but have different ideas of how you should live your life. You are thirty years old. It is time for you to stop letting your family control your life and for you to start making decisions that are best for you."

Michelle made more excuses in a few minutes than anyone else I have ever heard and ended with, "But my family expects me to be there. I can't go against their wishes."

Wow, because of what *they* want, she is going to sacrifice her happiness and sanity. This isn't about being nice or doing something to please someone; they are literally making her sick. I suggested to her to make her visits very short and set up ground rules if she needs to. Next year, go visit them for only a day during vacation week. And pick a day that they are all doing a group activity so that the conversation is limited.

After a few more visits with her family and coming home depressed and feeling worthless from their verbal beat-down she started limiting her time with her family. She was now ready to make a change and she prepared some comments to set the stage for her family. When her mom would start about marriage, she said, "Mom, I am happy being single and I am not going to settle for a man who doesn't love me and make me feel great about myself. Do you really want me to jump into a bad marriage?" When dad would disrespect her with comments about getting a real job, she responded, "Dad, not everyone gets a corporate job. I love helping people learn good food from bad food and live healthy long lives so that they can enjoy their grandchildren and great grandchildren." Her parents stopping giving her a hard time and respected her decisions. They just needed to understand why she lived differently than they expected.

Unless you are willing to do something different than you have done in the past, you will always get what you've always got. Are you going to live a life of mediocrity or poverty because those around you would rather grab your legs and pull you down than reach up to the rim of the pot? Or are you going to break free, shake the crabs off your ankles and become the one that paves the way for others?

The high road will become the example for your friends and family to emulate.

How To Get More

What if you want more than those who are around you? What if you want to become someone else? What if you are the positive one in your family and group of friends and it drives you crazy to be around them? Someone who is fat and wants to lose weight and get fit is going to have a really hard time making it happen if she is hanging out with people whose lives revolve around food. We all know people like this. Your family might even be like this. When I was a boy, on the Italian side of my family every special occasion had to have a huge meal. Sometimes the special occasion *was* the meal. Regular occasions had to have oversized meals and snacks could have been a dinner for three. Life revolved around meals.

My aunt's favorite household word was *mangia,* meaning enjoy the food and eat more. It was more of a command that a request coming from the lady in the moo-moo. My aunts and uncles who couldn't fit through a doorway without turning to the side would chastise my parents that I was too thin and they were not feeding me enough. Not exactly role models of fitness and health. Nonetheless, they were family and I loved them. It always made me laugh when my family watched football. They would yell and scream at the TV, "Come on you fat bastard, get the train off your back and catch the ball!" or "If you were any slower, I could beat you down the field!"

Luckily for me, we would visit only on the holidays and the influence was limited. If this were your family, you would grow up in an environment where food was valued highly because the food had the meaning of family, love, fun, and the spirit of the holidays. To not eat like them, you were disrespecting the family. They might even interpret your actions as "I don't love you" or "I am better than you." If your values are fitness and wellness, then you have to either limit your exposure to that environment or be ready to live your life on your terms even when your family gives you *agita.*

Control Your Environment

Do you want to be successful? Do you want to be lean, fit, and energetic? Do you want to live a life with people who support you and inspire you? Then you must *control your environment.*

You must control who has access to your mind and emotions by making intentional choices on what enters your mind. Like a cup can be filled with water, coffee, tea, juice, trash, or boogers, your mind is going to get filled with something.

If you don't choose, others will choose for you.

It's easy to control your environment. Go to places that are useful and empowering and don't go to places that are lethal to your success and happiness. An alcoholic who wants to stop drinking doesn't belly up to the bar and ask the regulars for advice. He would go to an AA meeting to be around people who have a vested interest in his success. If you are on a weight loss plan, going to an all-you-can-eat buffet is bad. Going to an organic health café would be good. Want to meet intellectuals? A book club might be inspiring. Going to see a live Jerry Springer show will not.

That's easy but what about family gatherings and holidays? How do you control those environments? With a little bit of planning and foresight, that can be easy too. If your family is typical, there are many negative toxic people you were blessed to share your bloodline. Lucky you. On big events that you cannot avoid, seek out the people who share the most in common with you and control the dialogue.

You can always say, "I would love to come to the Memorial Day barbeque Aunt Sophie, but I have this big project for work that I must get finished. Make sure you hug everyone for me." Sweet and honest. If you are an achiever, there is always something important for you work on. Your family will say something like, "Oh that girl is always working."

If you have to attend an event that is filled with people who are negative, complainers, tormenters, ridiculers and dream killers, then you must have a force-field. Just like on *Star Trek* or *The Incredibles*. Go to events knowing that you have to have your guard up and you will have to purge the negative energy when you leave. Plan your responses to the typical annoying comments in advance.

Do a cleansing raindance before you get back in your car. Jump up and down, hoot and holler and let those vibes and negative voodoo stay where they came from. Okay, so this is a little tongue in cheek. But not much. And if this works, do the dance. Your family thinks you're nuts anyway.

The Friend List

You must fire your loser friends. Don your hazmat gear and decontaminate your life from toxic sludge people. Unfriend on Facebook, break the connection on LinkedIn, don't StumbleUpon them, and purge them from your life.

Does this sound mean or selfish? Toxic people do not care about you and are not real friends. If they were, they would inspire you and support your growth. Some people are happy complaining, commiserating, bitching, moaning and groaning. Let them hang with others who share those values.

We have windows and doors with locks to keep people out of our home unless they are invited. You must do the same with your mind and emotions. Invite and surround yourself with friends and family who support you. Allow people to bend your ear who have your best interest at heart and want you to create the life that you want, not what *they* want. Ask advice from people who you admire, value, and respect their opinion.

Everyone has an opinion and they are going to tell you about it whether or not you ask for it. So choose to be around people who you might actually want to hear what they think and have worthwhile comments.

Mastermind Group

How much different would your life be if you got together with a group of like minded achievers who encouraged you to achieve more, offered advice and support, and held you accountable? Welcome to your *mastermind group*.

Mastermind groups tend to be a group of four to six people from various backgrounds for one central purpose – to help each other become more successful. Groups typically meet one to four times a month to challenge each other to create and implement goals, brainstorm ideas, and support each other with honesty, respect and compassion. It is a peer group of successful people coaching each other to amplify successes and minimize failures.

Being part of a mastermind group is like having a personal board of directors with the agenda on everyone's success as they individually define it. And it is like having an accountability board, a success team, and a peer advisory group, all rolled into one. Members are individually accountable and self-starting as well as team players.

In other words, be willing give as much as you receive.

Here are some of the things you may get out of a mastermind group. You can achieve more, be held accountable for goal/outcome setting, priority management, and the strategies you are using. You get differing perspectives, experienced advice, round robins feedback, and creative strategy sessions. In a great group you will be called on your B.S. You will learn as much from what you give to help others as you do from what you receive. It creates a synergistic atmosphere that fosters growth and achievement. With the right members it can be business coaching on steroids.

Fill Your Mind With Power

Did you catch the story about the boyfriend who left the girlfriend and stiffed her out of his half of the rent and now she is suing him and they are slandering each other on *Judge Jerk*? On the cable news the political left is badmouthing the right; the political right is ridiculing the left. It never stops.

You can choose powerful, enlightening, and positive information that will fill your mind with the fuel that empowers you to excel. If you are going to listen to something, you might as well listen to something that is going to improve your life. Get audio and video programs by the great masters. Fill your mind by reading great books and biographies.

My favorites are:

- Tony Robbins for success psychology
- T. Harv Eker and Marshall Sylver for money psychology
- Simon Sinek for business acumen
- Joel Osteen, Dr. Wayne Dyer and Deepak Chopra for spiritual enlightenment
- Seth Godin and for business thinking
- Les Brown for motivation
- Napoleon Hill and Jim Rohn for timeless success principles
- Craig Valentine for Story Telling
- Darren LaCroix & Ed Tate for business of speaking
- Stephen Covey for life principles
- Malcolm Gladwell for business philosophy.

This is a short list. For more suggestions go to http://www.DreamBigActBig.com/FillYourMind.

My iPod is filled with hundreds of audio books and seminars. Seriously, it is. I am always filling my mind with the ideas and thoughts of the best thinkers, living and dead. Every ultra-successful person I know and admire does the same thing. They cannot get enough of the minds of other masters. If there were a way to inject the information with an I.V. directly into our veins, we would do it because it is that important.

A College Education Without School

Imagine getting a college education's worth of knowledge without making time to go to college. No studying, no online courses, or dedicated time. It's easy. And if you are not doing it, you are missing out on of the greatest opportunities to learn and make an otherwise mundane task interesting. I have heard it called NET time or No Extra Time. This is any time that you can have an audio program playing in the background. Driving in your car, waiting in line, exercising, working in your house, or while watching the sunset.

You don't have to take notes, although that will help, and you don't have to even pay that close attention. Even if it is just in the background as noise, it will fill your subconscious mind and some of it will take root in your awareness. This is especially important to keep your mind from wandering into the mental car crashes when you are doing something mundane.

YOUR DREAM IS IMPOSSIBLE!

NOT! Failure is not trying. Failure is not getting back up after you've been knocked down or rejected. The quickest way to failure is to listen to others' small-minded comments or limited beliefs.

People believe what is possible for *you* by what they believe is possible for *them*.

Don't EVER let anyone tell you that your dream is impossible! Nobody! Not your friends, not your parents, not your brother, sister or grandma. Certainly not that schmuck boss, or that narrow-minded teacher you once had. Not that pathetic boyfriend or girlfriend whom you never should have dated in the first place. Not that moron critic or the town gossip. *Nobody.* Most importantly, don't ever listen to yourself when you hear those words of self-doubt creep out of the darkness of your mind.

You can do anything. You can become anybody. You can have it all. And I mean it all! There are no limitations in life except the limitations that you allow others to put on you or the limitations that you put on yourself.

It is up to *you* to move past the critical people and become what you were meant to be.

It is imperative that *you* rise above the circumstances of your past.

It is up to *you* to act even when you are terrified.

It is up to *you* to push through the discomfort to go further and harder than anyone else.

It is essential that *you* stand out above the crowd to be the example for others to set the mark by which to live by. It is up to *YOU*!

In the end you have only two people to answer to. Your creator and yourself. When it's your judgment day, you will look back and have to ask yourself, "Did I do all that I was capable to do?" Or will you stand proudly face-to-face with God and say, "I was everything that you gave me the ability to be. It is my gift to you and my gift to me and my gift to humanity."

Growing up I was taught that there is an afterlife. A Heaven, a glorious life where there is no pain, no disease, no heartache – a perfect place that is a reward to those who believe. But what if isn't exactly that way? What if this is your only chance? What if the proof of admission into Heaven is what you did here? Not only your beliefs – that's a given. What if your admission through the pearly gates is how you helped others? How you touched the hearts and emotions of strangers? How much good you have done in the world, making it a far better place than when you got here? What if you are judged by how you were able to provide for you family, your community, and for those who cannot provide for themselves?

Superstars think and make decisions based on how can they can help others and help themselves in the process. True superstars think and act beyond themselves.

The old way of thinking was to make a product, create the desire, and sell it. It has been going on since before the Industrial Revolution.

It didn't matter if it was good for humanity, only that it sold. And so, we ended up with fast food that will clog your arteries, and infomercials selling useless and falsely advertised junk.

The new and enlightened way of creating wealth is to create products that will help others. Ones that will empower others and are needed.

You might even say – products with a conscience.

Your dream is possible and it is exclusively up to you to make it happen. When you make your dream bigger then yourself, and make it about helping others or a greater cause, you will have so much more motivation, stamina, and enthusiasm to play at your highest level. It will no longer be a job because it will become a crusade.

Your Amazing Gift

We each have an amazing gift. We are all capable of so much more that what we have done until this point. You are remarkable and you're capable to make a lasting and massive impact on the world. What is that thing that you are specifically designed to do? How are you uniquely capable to touch others or this world is a spectacular way? Have you asked yourself these questions? I mean truly asked and thought about the answers?

If you don't know what your exceptional purpose or talent is, then keep asking yourself these questions over and over until they drive you insane to find a solution. The reason that you can't find the answer to these questions is because you are not asking yourself in a way that compels your unconscious mind to find the answer.

Ask yourself these questions to find your purpose:

What am I great at?
What do I love to do?
What is my special gift?
What is my unique personality trait?

What would I do if failure were not an option?

How can I help others and make this world better?

How can leave a legacy?

How do I want to be remembered?

Write these questions and answers down in a journal. Then keep building on your answers. Your gift is in the commonality of your answers. Your gift is what excites you the most.

Do you realize that nobody will remember you? Not even your family. In two or three generations you will only be a name on a family tree. Does this bother you? It should. It should tick you off. You may be mad at me for saying it or you may be mad at your no-good rotten grandkids who didn't keep your story alive. But you know what? It is not about them. It is about you. It is up to you to live a life so worthy, so extraordinary, and so legendary that your family will always remember you and so will the world.

You are the next Leonardo DaVinci, William Shakespeare, Henry Ford, Amelia Earhart, Emily Dickinson, John F. Kennedy, Neil Armstrong, Bruce Springsteen, Danica Patrick, Will Smith or [insert your hero here]. You are a star and your name should be included in a list like this.

I was listening to an audio book on success in my car, like I frequently do. It was a modern day motivational and personal development speaker and he was listing off many the most influential personal development people living and past. It was an all-star line up, "Napoleon Hill, Norman Vincent Peale, Jim Rohn, Dale Carnegie, Zig Ziglar, Tony Robbins, Brian Tracy, and Croix Sather."

Yes – me.

Okay, he didn't actually say my name, but that is what I heard. I don't know who the last person is on that list because every time I listen to it, I hear my name as the anchor name.

That was a turning point in my life because I knew that I was every bit as capable as any of them. It was my lack of action, my self-doubt, and creating excuses not to follow my dream that kept me from being on that list.

You must first *imagine* it.

Then you must *believe* it.

Then you must *achieve* it.

I already had the knowledge and experience, but I was missing a keystone until that point – an unwavering belief that I was designed to be on that list. Once I acknowledged and embraced this belief then the only thing I needed to do to become a world-recognized educator of personal empowerment was to take massive action and consistently move toward my dream. Once I did, my dream starting to become a reality. It was shortly after this that I came up with *Dream Big Act Big – Run Across America.*

Some people *teach* ideas and strategies. Others *live* them. The run is my way of living it and proving that anything is possible. When I started to tell people about my crusade, doors opened and people entered my life that could help. Was it luck or fate that World Ultrarunning Champion Stu Mittleman was coming to New York City a few weeks later?

I saw his event on Facebook and I signed up for Stu's training class in Central Park. I told him about my plans to run from coast to coast and invited him to dinner. He accepted and we had a great meal. We became instant friends. I asked him to mentor me for my run across America and he agreed. Stu is an amazing guy and absolutely brilliant. In addition to being a multi-time world champion inducted into American Ultrarunning Hall of Fame, he is also highly recognized for his nutrition expertise. Check out his book *Slow Burn*. The stories of his runs are incredible and the teachings of health, nutrition and running are priceless.

When I committed to running across America, people have been excited to help. Many have offered their services and offered financial support the cause. You can still help me make a massive impact on the world by going to HYPERLINK "http://www.DreamBigActBig. com"www.DreamBigActBig.com with your financial support by clicking on "sponsor" or "donate." The cause does not stop with the run – it will continue on for generations. The outpouring of love and support is amazing when you have a compelling idea and are taking massive action to make it happen. This will happen for you as well when you find your compelling future. Doors will open up to you in ways that will surprise you.

Who are your heroes? New York City Mayor Rudolf Giuliani has an insatiable need to read the biographies of baseball stars and great politicians. Lessons he learned from many of them (I am assuming the politicians) helped him make decisions while he was mayor. Every great achiever has studied other great achievers of today and of the past. The reason Mayor Giuliani will be remembered in history is because he expected no less of himself. He will always be credited with being the mayor who cleaned up New York City.

Make a list of the people whom you admire and that you dream to have a life like theirs. As you write out that list, put your name at the end. Then read that list out as if you are being introduced to an audience of your adoring fans. Or have a friend with a great voice record it for you so that you can make it your theme introduction and replay it when you need motivation.

STOP THINKING SMALL!

Thinking small sucks! You know someone who thinks small. You probably know hundreds of people who think small. Maybe you have been a victim of thinking small from time to time. Thinking small keeps people broke. Thinking small keeps people in a job that they don't like. Thinking small is buying into the idea that retirement is a prize. It is something that you get after slaving for an unappreciative employer for forty years to get a "Happy Retirement" cake, a tiny pension, and then having to watch your pennies and dimes to live out the rest of your years in a rocking chair.

Living your dream is the prize. Making an impact on others and a difference in the world are the prizes. Having a rich life filled with love, happiness, friends, adventures and wealth are the prizes.

> *"Only as high as I reach can I grow, only as far as I seek can I go, only as deep as I look can I see, only as much as I dream can I be."*
> – Karen Ravn, author.

Nothing great was ever achieved by thinking small. You never hear about manufacturing plant employee 4549 who works the graveyard shift, eats at the luncheonette every day, and dreams of writing a book – but never does. You never hear about the guy who opens up a hamburger joint and is the cook, cashier, and dishwasher. We don't hear about the talented high school athlete who doesn't get into college because he or she didn't work as hard on their grades as they did on the court. The people we hear about are the Danielle Steels, the Ray Krocs, and the Venus Williams of the world. We hear about the people with the big dreams and taking big actions to make life happen on their terms. These are the people who inspire us.

There is nothing wrong with thinking small if that is what you want. I haven't met many people who choose and enjoy small. Most people justify it. Most people want a bigger life. Most people want more. Most people want to do something great. You want more and that is why you are reading this book right now instead of watching the boob tube. Become the example of an extraordinary life.

Dream Big!

When you were a child you would lay on the grass, look up at the white clouds against the deep blue sky, and dream. One day you were going to be a doctor, a professional baseball player, then a firefighter, and then you would become an astronaut. Everything was possible because it was your dream and you could make it come true.

The greatest of mankind's accomplishments has been built on big dreams. Not just any dream, but *BIG DREAMS*. The most notable accomplishments in history were so big that the ideas were considered impossible. The automobile, plane flight, color television, personal computer, walk on the moon, women's suffrage, equal rights, and the first black United States President are just a few of the spectacular realities sparked by a dream. You can Google it and read it on Wikipedia to see if it is true. The most unbelievable dream at the time and one of the most amazing dreams in history was a man who said, "I have a dream."

America was discovered and then built by the biggest dreamers. How could you get a ship full of men and a Queen to fund a voyage that on every previous attempt everyone else had failed at or died on, if you didn't have an amazing dream? Ever since that first ship touched these shores, America has spawned countless dreams. What was once science fiction is now reality. Surgery by robots and cameras that you swallow were once thought ludicrous. People risk their lives everyday just to come to the United States for the opportunity to make their dreams come true.

Big dreams – I mean really, really, big audacious dreams – are endangered. They are at risk of becoming extinct. They will disappear like the dinosaurs and the rain forests if we keep subscribing to the ridiculous social constructs "to have a realistic goal" that we were taught as children. We are even taught to have achievable and measurable goals in business today. We are destined for mediocrity and losing our place as the land of opportunity if we continue to accept mediocrity as acceptable.

In the nineteen-forties, fifties, and sixties we were taught to go out and accomplish the American dream. Get a job with Big Blue or the Big Three, work hard, buy a house with a picket fence, settle down, and have 2.4 children. That was a great dream then. *That* American dream is now dead! *That* American dream no longer exists. It has been gone for decades, but nobody is talking about it. The big corporations are constantly outsourcing and restructuring. Schools are handcuffed by budgets and government regulations. And we are in a new economy. There is nothing wrong with our economy. We grew too big and now we adjusted. This is the new economy. Blaming the last administration or blaming the current administration is not going to help. Are you going to participate in the so-called recession? Are you going to wait for something that is probably not going to happen? Or will you refuse to participate and make your own economy and your own financial future and create the life of your dreams?

A person who fails to seize an opportunity has no advantage over the person who has no opportunity.

CAN YOU SEE YOUR FUTURE?

What gets you up in the morning? Is it the obnoxious buzz of your alarm clock or is it the thrill of a compelling future?

My daughter was so excited to be going to the zoo for the first time, as only a four-year-old can express. She could hardy go to sleep the night before. Finally she drifted off to sleep from shear exhaustion. In the morning she would typically wake up around eight. The morning she was going to the zoo was a very different story. "Daddy, daddy, are you awake yet?" I was because I heard her stampeding into the room. I pretended I was still sleeping. She waited for a minute wandering around the bedroom and pacing. Then she came back, "Daddy are you awake now?" with the voice of insistent fortitude. I figured I should respond before she got too ambitious and wake me on her terms. "Daddy, is the zoo open yet? Can we go now?"

"Good morning sweetie," I said. "I know you're excited, but it's only six in the morning. The zoo won't be open for hours."

My little four-year-old girl had a compelling future that morning. She knew what her day would be like and she was ready to make it happen even if the world wasn't just yet. What gets you excited?

What gets you up early in the morning? Make your dreams happen even if others aren't ready for it yet.

Most people go through life without a compelling future, without direction or even a destination other than two weeks a year vacation and some day, retirement. To have an exciting future you must see that exciting future before it is real. You must see it so clearly that it happens. This complements and fuels the chapter *What You Focus On Expands*. With a foundational focus of gratitude, opportunity, and positive expectancy, then you must design your compelling future. Something so exciting that you become a four-year-old little boy or girl wanting to go to the zoo or Disneyland. The world is your amusement park.

I know how easily you can fall into complacency and procrastinate. I know because I am the same way – if I do not purposefully act otherwise. Most humans are the same way. Luckily for us we have to ability to be more and do more if we choose. It is what makes us different from every other animal on the planet. If not we would have went extinct like prehistoric man. Ambition is taught and learned, not innate ability. However, laziness and doing the minimum is inherent. Recognize that your default mechanism is to do as little as possible. Recognizing that others are going to do as little as possible and expect the same of you will help you avoid that trap. I have also found that the *cost* of doing as little as possible, the *cost* of procrastinating, the *cost* of not doing what is necessary to create the life of your dreams is far more expensive than what it takes to live up to your potential.

Seeing your future is the first step to making a life beyond measure. Those who pause to see their future are the only ones that create their future. Everyone else has the future happen to them. Seeing your future is easy when you pause to create it. It may not come naturally at first, but in very short time, you can see the movie on your head in an instant.

In a moment I am going to ask you to do an exercise. It will be easy to justify *not* doing this exercise with an excuse like, "I know what I want." Before you skip this exercise let me ask you – How has your way been working so far? Successful people play full out and do whatever it takes to make it happen.

Rub The Lamp

In the fable *Aladdin*, he rubs an old tarnished lamp, smoke rises out of the lamp and then a genie appears to grant any three wishes. That story would be horrible if were true. You only get three wishes? What's up with that? In life you get as many wishes as you want. You are the magic genie and you can grant all the wishes you want. It is true. If you don't believe it, that will also be true – *for you*!

We are going to rub the lamp. Read this next paragraph, then put down this book and do the exercise. Your life depends on it! If you don't you will be subjected to life of mediocrity and regret. Then come back and finish reading.

Put on some nice easy instrumental music – something that you might hear in a sound track of a movie such as "Marian at the waterfall" from *Robin Hood, Prince of Thieves* or *Forrest Gump* "Suite" (of course there is a *Forrest Gump* song in my life). Grab a notepad or journal and sit in a comfy chair. Start writing down all of the things you want in life. Don't judge, filter, or stop – just write, write, write! Start with,

> "*In my life I will manifest this or something better…* "

Use as much detail as possible. Don't just write "Mercedes," write "black on tan Mercedes CLS550." If you don't know the details, write "black on tan Mercedes luxury sedan."

Not "a beach house" – "a 12,000-square-foot Mediterranean-style beach house on the southern California coast and my neighbor is a famous author."

Not just "a husband" – "My husband is young-forties, six feet tall, athletic build, financially independent, and shows me love by giving me a long hug and kiss every morning before we start our day and calls me *the one he has always waited for.*"

Keep writing for at least fifteen minutes non-stop. Don't filter, just write.

When you're finished, write at the bottom of the page,

> *"I am grateful for all of the wonderful people, adventures and things in my life now and what is coming to me in the future, in return I will give massive value to others."*

Then sign and date it and come back to reading this book to finish designing your life.

You have to imagine your future and all of its possibilities. Some of your dreams and desires will come to you by chance, some by fate, and some with purposeful and massive action. In reality it all happens because of you and the actions you take. It starts with imagining it and seeing it and wanting it and writing it down.

You will not find a mate by sitting at home like a hermit. You have to get out there to meet people. You will not sell books, find new clients, or buy investment homes by just imagining it. You are the spark, the fuel, and the fire. However, it all begins with you and inside of you.

It is easier to be guided though a *vision session*. In my seminars, the vision session is always the part that people love the most. If you want to do this with me, you can come to one of my weekend seminars. You will also learn how to create a burning desire that fuels your soul to make life happen like in your visioning session. To get you started, go to www.DreamBigActBig.com/myLife and get a free audio download of a vision session you can do at home.

Vision Boards

D. Mark Wheeler created a fabulous *vision board* at a workshop taught by Angela Lussier, author of the *Anti-Résumé Revolution*. In the workshop his vision board came to life with amazing photos, headlines, and text. It had a ton of emotional appeal to Dave and his vision board even inspired·others, including me.

On his vision board Dave had pictures of people he wanted in his life, experiences, accomplishments, and things. He had the words *Entrepreneur of the Year*. He also had a cartoon dog. He didn't know why that should be on there, but he knew there would be a dog in his future.

Less than a year later Dave started a new company called WheelDoggy.com and the company logo is of a green cartoon dog that he commissioned. The WheelDoggy concept is connecting people that need something done with people who have the talent to get it done. Accolades are certain to be in his future.

Vision boards are typically created by cutting out magazine photos and words, and pasting them to a poster board. They can also be so much more. Dave scanned his photos and uses them as a screen saver on his computer. I started a vision board on my FaceBook account. You can see it at http://www.Facebook.com/Croix. You can also post photos on your bathroom mirror so you see it every night and morning like I do. Some people create scrapbooks as if the life they want has already happened. Need some ides? Google *vision board images* to get thousands of examples. The possibilities are only limited by your imagination. Do you have an amazing vision board that has been inspired by this book? Go to www.DreamBigActBig.com/visionboard to upload your vision board to inspire others.

What's important on a vision board? Make it personal and motivating. It must evoke emotion within you. When you look at it, it should electrify you as if you are listening to *Eye of the Tiger*. It should be placed or hung somewhere you can see it every day. Look at it with gratitude for what you have and what will enter into your life. Know that all of these images and words will come true *or something better.*

Imagining your future, vision sessions, and vision boards – do they really work? Yes, it works because your brain is designed to see in images. It is how we learn language and most everything we do. Images evoke emotions and emotions control your life. Think of a photo of 9/11. Nearly any photo of the Twin Towers tragedy will get you tear or gape. Now think of a photo of an athlete crossing the finish line with their arms up to the sky and breaking the finish ribbon. That makes you smile. Especially if you think of a time when you were the winner crossing the finish line. Think of a photo of when your baby was born, or an awesome vacation. Think of your wedding photos – those may make you tear in happiness or tear in sorrow. Images create emotions. These are nothing more than paper and ink, or just imagined. And yet they can strike up an overwhelming reaction within you. Life is determined by emotions, so the stronger the emotion and more vivid the images the faster and easier your life by design will come to you.

Here's why – your mind does not know the difference between what is real and what is imagined. A vividly imagined reality will create and cause the same physiological, biological, psychological and emotional effects as a real occurring event. Remember a time when you thought someone had done something to wrong you. You got so mad you were ready to redesign his face . Then it turned out that it never happened. You had wrong information. You imagined something to be real and you reacted as if it were real, but it wasn't.

What you believe to be true is true for you.

Another example: there are many people who are intensely afraid of snakes. It's called ophidiophobia. For some of you reading this, the word "snake" makes your heart race.

Do you know what's interesting? Often people who are afraid of snakes have never even met a snake. It's an irrational fear. In any one year in America, only five people die from snakebite. You are thirty times more likely to be killed by a *deer* than a *snake*. And yet ophidiophobia is totally real. For some people the mere event of seeing a photo of a snake will send panic coursing through their veins. For famous award-winning actress S. Epatha Merkerson, she had a panic attack when watching a sci-fi T.V. show. "I won't even read a script with a snake in it," she confessed, "That's the first thing I asked when they send it [the script] over," according to a BVBUZZ.com article.

What you imagine is real for you. Imagine something intensely enough and your mind will believe it is real, because it now is. Athletes use imagination and visualization when they compete. Racers see themselves crossing the finish line first, springboard divers see their dive happening to perfection, and performers see a perfect dance, or hear a perfect rendition before walking on the stage. I saw myself successfully finishing my run across America thousands of times in my mind before that day would happen.

What does this mean to you and how can you harness the power of your imagination? Visualize your life, your future and your dreams with intense vivid, frequent imagery plus emotion, and they will come true. Imagine and visualize yourself as confident, act as if you are confident, and you will *become* confident. In your visualization, see yourself walking with full confidence. Notice how you breathe. Experience the emotion of confidence when standing tall, asking and getting what want. Hear others tell you, "I love your confidence. It is wonderful to meet a person who knows what she wants." Then each time you are walking, move with that confidence that saw in your mind's eye. Head up, chest slightly lifted, breathing deeply, and moving gracefully.

At first it might be a challenge to visualize your future in your mind. With regular practice, it will come naturally. Practice daily before you go to bed. Use down time to practice, like when you are stuck waiting for an appointment. If I'm stuck in the waiting room before my next appointment, I will sit upright, with my hands resting on my knees, head looking straight, and I close my eyes. I then start to visualize how I want the meeting to end, how the week should go, or something else that is happening in my life. Sometimes I am asked, "Croix, are you awake, we are ready to see you now." I just smile. If prompted I will say that I was meditating. That usually gets me the "Oh, okay" look and everyone goes on their way.

MAKE THE LEAP

If you catch a grasshopper and put him in a glass jar with the top on, he will jump and jump and jump and keep banging his head. Let him do this for a couple of days then take the top off. Most grasshoppers will not jump out and be free.

When we are children and throughout college, many of us are in a glass jar with a lid. Someone else is always telling where our ceiling is. What is possible and impossible, and most of us take the guidance as fact. Then the top is taken off the jar. Most people stay in the jar by getting a job that pays the bills. The few that jump out become the Steve Jobs, the Oprahs, and Bruce Springsteens.

You'll never hear a person on their deathbed saying, "I wish I played it safe. I wish I tried fewer things. I wish that I took fewer risks. I wish I experienced less. I wish my life was boring and I unfulfilling." Nobody would ever say that. People always wish they had more, done more, tried more, experienced more.

We always believe that we will have more time to get to our dreams. When the kids are older, when I get twenty years at my job and am vested I will quit, when the economy gets better, when... when... when.

When will it happen if it doesn't happen today? For many people tomorrow never comes. My friend's athletic and strikingly fit daughter died of cancer at twenty-six. My uncle died in his thirties, my aunt in her forties, and my friend and volunteer firefighter at thirty-eight from a freak accident. You probably have some people in your life who passed away too young.

My older brother Darrin had just turned forty-four when he decided to go back to school. He was in a lot of physical pain from working construction all his life and from a bad construction accident that had broken his back. Darrin wasn't sure what he wanted to do, but he was certain that he needed to make a change because the life he was living was literally killing him. When September arrived he started his classes. He was very proud for finally moving forward to make a different and better life for his wife and fourteen-month-old son.

Shortly after Darrin went back to school, I got a call one morning from my father. "Darrin is dead," he said, crying.

"Who? You mean my brother?" I barked back in disbelief. It was my brother and we had to go immediately to the hospital to see him for the last time. Why does this happen? Why does someone die so young? It's not fair and it's not right.

It could be me, or could be you, or someone you love. You never know when your time will end. Darrin died of a massive heart attack at forty-four. No warning, no chance to say goodbye. It is sad and feels unfair. The only thing I can do is move forward and let the best of my brother live on through me. My brother was my idol growing up and now he is my guide. Everywhere I go a part of Darrin goes with me, shaping my life as if he were here giving me advice.

I got a gift in my brother's sudden passing. A lesson I unfortunately didn't learn when he was alive and wish I did, but could only learn in this time of tragedy. This lesson is what inspires me to move forward bravely with my brother in my heart and influencing my decisions.

He loved people in a way few people do or can. His life was about connecting and making others happy. His life was about family and friends and sharing. He served people and brought beauty into their day with his smile and infectious laugh. Despite his back pain he would rise though the anguish and offer the only thing he had to give some days – his smile and words of cheer.

What a beautiful world this would be if more people gave away a smile and a laugh with reckless abandon.

What are you waiting for? Seriously – what the hell are you waiting for? Make your life happen today. Stop waiting, stop believing those ridiculous imaginary excuses and you have been telling yourself and make your life happen on your terms. Do it for yourself, your family, your friends, and for the world. You are an amazing and beautiful person. It is selfish to play life small and rob the world of the gift you have. Make the leap and take a step forward and continue forward with the resolve of a stampede of wild stallions until you create a life better than a fairy tale.

GOOD IS THE ENEMY OF GREAT

When you are willing to accept good, great becomes impossible. Good is easy. Good doesn't require much effort. Good can be attained by anyone with just the littlest bit of effort. It is easy to stop at good. At many jobs to be merely good is even expected and acceptable. But what does a good job pay? Crap! How does doing a good job feel? Like crap! What does a good job look like? Crap! So if your job and your production output feels like crap, looks like crap, and pays like crap, what kind of life are you going to have?

Often greatness falls victim to the constant rush of getting it done. I regularly see my corporate friends ready to pull their hair out because a client calls at four o'clock on Friday afternoon and needs a new project that day. For what? To sit in an email inbox until Monday, or Tuesday or Wednesday? Then several days later – after you worked until ten o'clock Friday night getting it done – the client emails you back and says, "Hey, I couldn't open the email. Can you resend it?"

Much of corporate America has gone to the world of *good enough*. It is not even a matter of status quo anymore; now it is figuring out how to reduce product quality to save cost and minimize customer loss. Because of this, you have an extraordinary opportunity to stand out as a superstar and WOW your clients.

When the world is becoming "good enough," go the extra mile and over-deliver. When the world never goes above and beyond the call of duty, do something to knock their socks off. Here is why. When you do more than your clients or customers expect, they are going to love you. They are going to talk about you. They are going to recommend you. They will become your raving fans.

My dad would tell me, "If you cut corners, your client will warn his friends about you. Do the minimum and he will tell nobody. Do your best work every time and he will become your cheerleader." Because of this advice I never needed to advertise when I was a home remodeling contractor, and I always had a waiting list of clients just like my father did. Always do your best, even if the customer won't see the difference in quality. Today, I never watch the clock with my hypnotherapy or coaching clients. We are together until we have achieved a desired result.

Those who have the attitude that "it's good enough," "that's not my job," "our forty-five minutes are up," or "someone else will fix it" will always get what they have always got. A wage-paying job that they hate. That's if they can find a job at all.

When you are very good you earn a good living, you might have a nice house with a little white picket fence, and maybe a 401k plan. When this happens many become complacent because it is *easy*. You have the same routine, the same standard of living you have had for the past ten years, the same vacations, and the same friends. You get a new econobox car every six or seven years and this seems nice. There are no surprises; it just works. Because it works, it's easy to rationalize and lose the desire to grow and achieve more.

Good is the enemy of great because when you have it good, why should you expect more? You have more than your parents ever did.

You have more then many of your peers and life is safe when it's good. You may even think that it's selfish and greedy to want more. I say it's selfish *not* to want more. It's selfish not to live up to your potential. You are depriving your family, friends, and the world of your abilities and talents. When you have more you can contribute to your community, church, those in need, by giving back more than others can. It's your responsibility to do the best you can. To create a life of adventure and then give back is a big way that blesses others and brings more blessings into your life.

Do you want sit in your rocking chair wishing you went on amazing vacations or do you want to reminisce about the African safari and the Pacific islands cruises while planning your next adventure? You deserve the luxurious home on a picturesque property that has a spa-like feel. Every day when you come home you should say to yourself, "My gosh, I am blessed to live in this home. Thank you." You should have the car that gets you excited to open the door and sit down in the plush seats and revs your heart as you rev up the engine. You are worthy of a relationship that lights you up like a fairy tale happily ever after. You were designed to have a career that makes you jump out of bed because you love what you do that much.

These are the things that greatness gives you. There are no exceptions. Great things come to those who give great value to that improves the lives of others. Great things come to those who are willing to go the extra mile giving more than what is asked of them with a smile and happy attitude. For those who are great, the national economy is a small factor in the money equation.

Masterpieces of art were never painted by someone who did a good job. Musical masterpieces were never written by a musician that did a good job. Movies that inspire you were never produced by a someone that did it good enough, and the lead roles were never played by actors who are mediocre.

"The only greatness for man is immortality"– James Dean.

Superstars always give more than that is asked of them. They always put in more effort, more time, and pay attention to the smallest of details. It is what distinguishes them from the rest. Tiger Woods will finish a PGA and then immediately go practice his swing. Looking for the smallest of improvements to give him an even better advantage. Singing legends Garth Brooks, Madonna, and Usher didn't get to where they are by stopping at good. They didn't become icons by pursuing little dreams; they went for the big dream. They focused, practiced, continually improved and followed their passion to be among the best in the world.

"Nobody will expect more of me than I expect of myself."
– Actor Will Smith

Superstars put in the time and the dedication before anyone has ever heard of them. Follow your dream and move toward your purpose with zeal and passion. Go to the best of your ability when nobody is watching. Move forward when people are still teasing you and telling you to give up on "your silly dream."

Be the Best in the World

In Seth Godin's book *The Dip* he talks about being the best in the world. On the surface that means being the very best. To be a Rembrandt, Beethoven, Shakespeare, The Beatles, Morgan Freeman, or Bill Gates.

Seth brings a distinction to that idea that is very important. He talks about being the best in *your* world. If you are a teacher, be the best teacher in your school district. If you are a pediatric doctor, be the best pediatric doctor in your town or county. Whatever it is that you do, be the best that you can be in *your* world.

After being hit by the drunk driver's car, I often headed down the road of trouble. Without swimming, I found other ways to feel significant. I went beyond doing stupid things like other teens. I pushed the envelope – right to the edge. I would go out and find cars with keys in the ignitions. I would take the cars out for joy rides for a while and then return them to the same spots that I found them. How confused would you be if you got into your car and the seat and mirrors were moved and the fuel gauge was lower? I'm sure a lot of people were scratching their heads trying to figure that one out.

One day a friend and I got caught up in the exciting idea that I would heist a brand-new car off a dealer's lot. On the very first lot I found a car with the keys in the ignition. The car had seven miles on it. I drove off the lot and then we pushed the envelope right off the table. I started ramming guardrails and driving off road. At one point I got the car to fly eight feet in the air. Think the car chases in the movies are unrealistic? Not so much. A few hours later the car is totaled by countless blunt trauma injuries.

They say timing is everything. This was certainly true in the wee hours of that morning. As we were about to abandon the car, a county police car came driving down the rural suburban road. "Damn, this isn't good." I thought. After a barrage of questions we slipped with our story. "Officer, we just stopped to see if anyone needed help," I stated.

"Then how did your sweatshirt get in the car?" the cop asked.

"I must have forgo ..." Doh! We were caught. The officer saw through our story immediately. It didn't take long before we were cuffed and in the back of his car.

I would have spent time in a juvee home or jail if my parents hadn't hired the best attorney in the region. Obviously we couldn't hire the best attorney in the *country*, but we could find the best in *our area*. It didn't take long to find him. My parents asked around and Kevin's name kept coming up over and over. He was the best in the world of criminal defense in the tri-county area. Friends, court clerks, cops, and even the talk at the coffee shop was to go find this legend. This guy was sharp and street smart. He knew the system and he knew how to get the best deal for his clients. And most everyone knew about him. To this day I still don't know how my parents afforded him. They paid the attorney and the restitution. If they didn't my life would be dramatically different. Guaranteed.

My punishment was one hundred hours of community service. I was sent to the Boys and Girls Club to be their manual laborer. At sixteen, manual labor is not appealing. Not even a little. But it was more appealing than the court's other options. The supervisor sent me out into the field and gave me a rake. I had three hours to work that afternoon. I don't know what got into me, but I raked as fast and as hard as I could and never complained. That is very unlike a sixteen-year-old. Especially this sixteen-year-old. I came back a couple of days later and did the same thing. I worked hard and nobody bothered me. On the third day the supervisor called me into his office. There were others in the room when I entered. I was thinking, "Come on, what more do they want from me? I'm busting my rear by being a human leaf blower."

"Young man, we've been watching you from these windows," the supervisor said.

I'm thinking I'm in trouble again. Maybe I was raking west when I should have been raking east or some other stupid adult rule.

"We rarely see a teen who works like you," the supervisor continued. "We didn't expect anything out of you except to fulfill your time for the court. We expected you to do as little as possible. You have pleasantly surprised us."

Tom , the supervisor, introduced the other people in the room and said, "This is Jen, the head of gymnastics; and this is Mike, head of equipment and facility maintenance." Tom looked at me. "Do you think you are working hard out there in the field?"

"I'm busting my butt – look at the blisters on my hands," I replied. "When I leave here I can barely lift my forearms up to my face to take a drink of water."

"Would you rather have a fun job inside? Tom asked. "Because if you're willing to work as hard as you did out there, you can finish your time for the court working as a gymnastics assistant for Jen, or you can be a mechanical assistant for Mike. Do either of these appeal to you?"

What is going on here? Is this possible, are they really offering me a sweet deal to play with kids in gymnastics, a sport that I loved and excelled at only second to swimming? Did they even know how much I loved gymnastics?

I wasn't going to argue and enthusiastically said, "I would love to be a gymnastics assistant. I love gymnastics and I am very good at it at my high school. But why? Why would you believe in me after the trouble I got into? The reason that I'm here is to do my community service time!"

"Listen kid, we all do stupid things, especially at your age," said Mike. "Stealing cars is stupid, but you are so much more than that. You went too far and now you're paying the price. Even as adults we find ourselves wishing we had made different choices. But your time here in the field, you didn't have to work hard. You didn't have to show up on time and give 110% with a rake in your hands. You showed us that you are different. You demonstrated that you want to excel."

"Croix, why did you take that car?" Jen interrupted. "To prove yourself?"

I wasn't sure how to answer so in a rare moment I stayed quiet and wondered why I did some things.

"I'm guessing that you wanted to feel alive, get a thrill, and feel important," Jen continued. "Do you realize what this means? You're a leader. You're willing to go where others will not go, and take chances. You can end up in jail, or it can lead you to an amazing life. Maybe head of a company or even your own company."

After a long pause Tom emphasized the point. "Croix, your life is in your hands. You can be a great failure or you can do great things."

"If I accept you as you are, I will make you worse; however if I treat you as though you are what you are capable of becoming, I help you become that" – Johann Wolfgang von Goethe, German playwright, poet, and novelist. 1749-1832)

I finished my community service time as a gymnastics assistant. At the end of the one hundred hours, they *hired* me to continue working in that position. I stayed with them for two seasons before moving on. This was one of my moments of living life as a superstar and making the best out of something unfortunate. I learned that giving your best is important no matter what you are doing. From raking leaves to being a parent, what ever it is that you are doing, do it well, or don't bother doing it at all.

ARE YOU INVISIBLE?

Zebras have black and white stripes for a very important reason. When zebras are threatened with an attack by a lion or other predator they immediately form a huge group and run around in that cluster. Because of their contrasting strips and the movement, the zebras blend in, making it confusing and the individual invisible. The lion has a very hard time picking out a single weak animal. If the lion cannot pick out a single zebra to tire out, then he has little chance of catching his lunch.

Those who follow the crowd are zebras in a sea of moving confusion. There's nothing wrong with being a zebra if you want to be a zebra. There's a lot wrong with behaving like a zebra when you are the lion, a elephant, or an eagle.

In a rare moment when I was mindlessly watching TV, I was flipping through the dial when a reality show caught my attention. Maybe it was the bikini-clad woman walking down the runway. The reality show was to find the next Latino model superstar. When she finished her walk the panel of judges tore her apart and sent her on her way. Ouch! The next model walked in, and this scene repeated itself every couple of minutes with varying levels of comical and rude comments from the panel of judges.

Most of the women were dressed like porn stars until one woman walked down the runway with an amazing smile and an outfit just as classy as her smile. She didn't have to say a word – you knew she had "it." What she had was style, confidence, charisma, and an understated sex appeal. Then she fielded the panel's questions as if she knew the questions in advance. She was intelligent, prepared, professional, and had a plan for her life. She stood out from all the zebras.

You will never get on *Oprah, Good Morning America,* or the *Tonight Show* if you are an invisible zebra. You are not going to get noticed for the promotion, get your resume to the top of the pile, or make it to the finals. Being invisible, being like everyone else, or following the crowd is *boring*. Being a zebra is *safe*. Being safe doesn't get you the big reward or the recognition.

My Zebra Book

It's a great book, but I made bad marketing mistake. My first book, *BetterBody BetterLife,* is lost in the sea of fitness books. Why? I didn't make it memorable. At that time I didn't know any better. That book is a zebra.

I believe it is one of the best books you will find on health, fitness, permanent weight loss, and living a vibrant life naturally without dieting. I spent years researching and writing the book for people who want a straightforward guide to living a healthy lifestyle. I made it simple to understand and easy to follow. Living a healthy life is actually easy and can be fun. Sounds great, right? You can find it at http://BetterBodyBetterLife.com. It's great, but it lacks the marketing pizzazz of more popular books. It doesn't matter how great my book is if too few people hear about it or find it. It doesn't matter how effective my fitness strategies are and if I get rave reviews from my clients if the book reviewers don't read my book. You have only a few seconds to capture the attention of your audience.

How many amazing, talented people were not discovered and lived in obscurity? There are so many. I meet so many people who are extraordinarily talented and have an amazing gift to give to others, but they never get out of their comfort zone to make a difference like they want. In the past that was me. So far, that has been *you* and millions of zebras like you.

If you got this far in this book, you are certainly not a zebra at your core. You may have been behaving like one.

Every time that you decide to wait until tomorrow, every time you don't make the important phone call, every time you don't take action, keep this visual in your mind. When you are standing still or when you are running around in circles doing meaningless to-do's, remember that in that moment you are dressed in a zebra outfit. The zebra outfits didn't work in the 1980s and they don't work now. Take the zebra skin off and do something that brings you closer to your goals. Do something that moves you towards a life of adventure. Do something that makes you more of the spectacular person you are and allows you to share your gift to the world. Do something that is going to get you noticed by your audience.

DREAM THE IMPOSSIBLE DREAM

Mega-hits happen so quickly because they have a compelling story. It's interesting, hilarious, emotionally moving, über-humanitarian, ridiculous, difficult, unbelievable, a new record, a new and unknown idea or act, or it's a great love story.

When you are boring you are unnoticed. Boldness is rewarded. Be bold, be daring, be different, or be amazing. Better yet, be all of it. My great friend Doug Comstock ends his emails with, "Go Big or Go Home." It's his saying that helped to spark my run across America. I got to thinking, "What is the biggest thing I can do at this stage in my life?"

Dream so big it seems impossible and then take action that makes it possible. What was science fiction a few decades ago is now reality. Space flight, deep-sea exploration, cloning, and global cell phones were all thought to be impossible. A key ingredient to my run across the country is that most people ask, "Is that even possible?" Every time I hear that question it excites me because the idea is astonishing.

We live in a culture that emphasizes instant gratification. Drive-thru meals, instant downloads of music, winning the lottery, and instant superstars from winning a reality talent TV show are ubiquitous.

Many want the same thing from their careers. It's possible to become a superstar in your arena in a very short time. To do that you must get noticed. I mean really noticed in a big way. There is a realtor in my area who advertises everywhere. Billboards, newspapers, and her mailings are almost inescapable. Her name is on "for sale" signs everywhere. She is considered the realtor expert. Not because she is any better than any other realtors, but because of her recognition. She also works hard to find leads and makes sales. So she actually is one of the best in the area. What is she doing in a big way? Getting out there in person and in advertising so that nearly everyone knows who she is. Because of it her checkbook is fat. She is the best in the world of the local real estate market.

I got a call from Andy, whom I knew through social circles. He wanted to become a professional speaker. We met at a nice American bistro, ordered our meals and a couple of beers in iced mugs.

"I speak regularly in front of large audiences," Andy began. "I have a good job. I like it some and I make enough money to pay for my mortgage, car payments, and for a vacation once a year with my wife and two kids. But I don't want to be a desk jockey for the rest of my life. I want to become a business coach and professional speaker. But how can I do that if I can't afford to leave my job? We only have a little bit in savings."

I explained to him how I got my speaking bookings and coaching clients. And then I told him, "Andy, if you want life to happen for you in a big way, you need to make a big move. Get your flyers, one-sheet, demo video, and website going. Then go out and hit the phones and knock on doors until you get your first three speaking jobs lined up. Then quit your job. That will equal three months salary. That's just one speaking event a month to replace your monthly income. What if you lined up two or three a month? You are immediately tripling your income and you will work less than you do now. How is that one-week vacation sounding now? Kinda lame, huh?"

On April 21, 1519 Conquistador Hernando Cortez landed his ships on the coast near Veracuz, Mexico. They unloaded the ships and stood as Cortez addressed them. He said something like, "Men, we are here to conquer this land. We are outnumbered three hundred to one. We can retreat and go back to Spain as failures, or we can take this land and be remembered for all time." It was at that moment that Cortez turned to the sea, facing his ships, and yelled, "Burn the ships!" The men on the ships did as he commanded and all of his ships burned into the water and sank.

His small group of men panicked and yelled, "Are you crazy? We will all die!"

Cortez turned back to his men, "We will conquer or we will die. Our ships are gone and we have only one option. We must be victorious. We can take control this land and take their ships back home where we will be welcomed as heroes."

Mega-success comes to those who burn their boats, making success the only possibility.

Read a biography of any historical or modern-day icon, and you will find that they had big dreams and went after those dreams by taking decisive action like Cortez. Martial artist and movie producer Bruce Lee didn't say, "I want to be an actor." He wrote a letter to himself dated January 9, 1970 that said,

"By 1980 I will be the best known Oriental movie star in the United States and will have secured $10 million dollars. And in return I will give the very best acting I could possibly give every single time I am in front of the camera and I will live in peace and harmony."

It was less than ten years before Bruce Lee exceeded his goals. He was committed to his goal. You can see his original signed letter at the Hard Rock Café in New York City.

Growing up in the construction trade and being very good at it, my failsafe was always that I could go back to being a carpenter. Then I said, "No more!" No more playing it safe, no more thinking small. I sold all of my tools, turned down every call that came in, and broke ties with the building industry. I stepped fully into coaching, speaking, and eventually into becoming an ultra-athlete.

It is easier to hold on to our crutches – like a dead-end secure job or a familiar but unfulfilling relationship – than to turn and run boldly towards our goals. Holding onto those things that are comfortable are the exact things that are going to keep you from becoming a superstar. Just like having one foot on the dock and the other foot on your boat. The only thing that is for certain is that you are going to get your ass in the water.

I've heard many creative excuses. "I'm too old, too young, there's big project at work, the house needed painting, the kids are off for summer break, the kids are going to college in the fall…" The excuses go on and on. You can't make a living by making excuses.

I didn't understand how some very big people succeeded until I read Sir Richard Branson's autobiography. Sir Richard is emblematic perfection of *Dream Big Act Big*. In *Losing My Virginity*, he retells one business adventure after another, risking it all over and over. Many times he went to the brink of no return only to come out bigger, better, and far richer. He is a billionaire, one of the richest people in the world, and he is dyslexic. Ironic, isn't it?

Shortly before I developed *Dream Big Act Big*, I was almost $1.4 million in debt. Far upside down in my debt-to-income each week, I wondered where I was going to beg, borrow, or steal the mortgage payment on one of the real estate properties I owned. I had always made money in real estate as a side business in the 1990s and 2000s and thought I could keep going with the same business plan. Then I made a couple of bad investments by buying houses that I should have stayed away from. I couldn't sell them and had everything mortgaged to the hilt. With housing prices still on the correction, I had to get out. Finally, I reduced the prices and sold everything but my primary home at a massive discount, and lost fifty thousand dollars.

It turned out to be a blessing. If I hadn't hit an extreme financial challenge, I would have continued on my complacent way. I wouldn't have decided to focus on my true passion, teaching from the stage as a public speaker. I would have kept dabbling in my passion because I was making money in real estate.

Stand Out and Get Rewarded

Why should you stand out? Those who stand out are rewarded hundreds of times more than those who have stopped at "good." Author Seth Godin describes it as "pushing through the dip," and author Malcolm Gladwell calls it "the tipping point." Most people stop in the dip or just before the tipping point. When this happens, those people stay in relative obscurity, meaning that few people hear about them. Only a few of those people will recommend them or talk about them. Only a few of those people they tell will act on their words and recommendations.

When you stay in the dip or you stay on the entry side of the tipping point, it is impossible to get to the situation where people seek you out. You never get momentum and you feel like you are always walking in deep mud. Every step is hard and monotonous.

Remember how much fun it was playing on the playground as a child? Go back to the time when you were on the seesaw. Up and down, up and down. That was fun when you had someone else to play with. One day you didn't have anybody to play with, but you tried. You sat on one side and pushed up, but each time you came back to your starting point. No matter how hard you pushed, you never got enough leverage to go up in the air like when you played with another child.

Then you decided to walk up one side of the seesaw and then back down the other side. You probably had your mom or dad yelling at you, "Don't do that, it's dangerous!" What happened? After you crossed over the fulcrum, the pivot point at the center, the seesaw breached the tipping point and then you walked down the other side. You then walked up and over several more times and laughed as you did it. That was one of the most important lessons you will ever learn and you had no idea that it meant anything.

When you're starting something new it is more difficult on the entry side of the seesaw than it is after you have passed the fulcrum. The seesaw tips and you start walking down. On the way up you are networking to find new clients, learning a new job, going through college, and going through the early parts of the learning curve. Once you cross over the tipping point, clients start calling you, people start talking about you, you are mastering your job, and you get to the part of the learning curve that feels comfortable.

Most people stop with one foot on either side of the fulcrum. This is called *complacency*. It's easy. You have enough clients to keep you afloat, you have enough proficiency that your job becomes easy, and you feel like you have succeeded. After all, you are no longer going uphill. This is a good place to be. Your income will never really be spectacular, but you will be comfortable. When you get here, you are further than so many other people. However, if you stop here, you will feel great for a while, but then one day you start to wonder, "Is there more?"

When you are running up a hill it takes a lot of effort to get up that hill. As you come close to the crest it is much easier. It feels as if you are running on flat ground. You have not reached the peak yet, so you are still going up hill. But in comparison to the incline, it is easy. Then you get to the true peak and it becomes even easier. You are still making yourself move forward. When the road starts to tip down, gravity helps you. You can dramatically pick up the pace, running faster with less effort. If the road gets a little steeper going downhill you will run faster with less effort.

It doesn't matter if you're walking up a seesaw, running up and over a hill, or starting a new job or a new business – once you get to the center it *feels* easier. Once you cross that tipping point it *becomes* easier. Once past the fulcrum you will reach a level of saturation in your market, and people will seek you out in droves. Clients will tell others and those people will tell others and they will tell others. People who aren't your clients but have heard about how great you are will tell other people.

Each small city has hundreds of defense attorneys. There is always one that stands out and is sought after and recommended the most. Attorney "Big" is on the news, in the newspapers, and is the talk of the coffee shops. Attorney Big is the one who goes after the high-profile cases. He or she may or may not be better than any other attorney, but they go after the *big cases*. When Attorney Big wins a high profile case, it's all over the news and it's the talk of the legal circles in the city. When someone asks, "Who is the best defense attorney in the city?" others will say, "Attorney Big just won the case for Infamous Jones." It doesn't matter what his or her winning ratio was before that case because they just won the biggest trial in recent history. Now Attorney Big has other high profile cases coming to their door and they get to pick and choose the cases they want and how much they will get paid. Attorney Big gets ten, twenty, maybe thirty times the income of any other attorney in town.

Rarely will you ever hear of the athlete who comes in second or third unless you are an avid fan of that sport. The athlete who wins the title also wins the big prize money, the big sponsorships, and the fame. The prize money and sponsorship difference between first place and second is not even close. First place leads to high-paying speaking engagements, book sales, and partnership offers. The rewards can be a hundred times bigger for first place than for second place. And if you are tenth, you get *bupkis.*

When you stand out, you will have few, if any competitors. The person who has the best resume will be added to the short list. When that same resume has an endorsement from a highly credentialed organization, that resume goes to the top of the short list. If that same person can interview very well, every other candidate is compared to him or her. When that person comes with a personal endorsement from a trusted friend or colleague, nobody else is considered.

Dream Big Act Big Run Across America was designed to make the event and me stand out. I am the only one ever to combine a 3,000-mile coast-to-coast run with an inspirational speaking tour. Nobody has ever done it and the chances of it being replicated are near zero. Why? Because few people on earth would consider running across America. Of those people who would consider it, few of them are charismatic inspirational speakers. Of those people who can run 3,000 miles and are great speakers, none of them are doing it – making my competition exactly zero.

That's not even the exciting part.

THE SELF-SABOTAGE CYCLE

The exciting part of my Run Across America is not the fact that I am running 3,000 miles in one hundred days. Or even the fact that I am the only one in the world to incorporate a speaking tour at the same time. Certainly those are both awesome feats. What excites me is the ripple effect that will be created. Like a pebble thrown into a pond that sends out waves of ripples, my *Dream Big Act Big* Run Across America will affect tens of thousands of lives. As the famous music conductor Benjamin Zander said, "My job is to awaken the possibility in others."

I hope the same thing happens to you that has happened to me. Your life can be radically shaped in an instant by an event, a conversation, a lesson, a story, a helping hand, a kind ear, a true friendship, and a loving heart. Many amazing people have dramatically shaped my life. If it were not for those amazing souls who saw the superstar-in-the-rough and reached out to help me, I could not have been able to rise above my past. I would not have been able to see the beauty inside me, embrace the belief that I am here for a purpose, and taken life-changing action to make it happen. If it were not for the lessons and strategies that I learned, I would have stayed in an endless cycle of self-sabotage. You can achieve and achieve and achieve. But if you have a program in your head that sabotages your success, your life will always be limited. This will frustrate you because you know you are capable of so much more, but you don't understand why you cannot break through. This chapter will help you find those limiting programs and show you how to break through to reach higher levels than ever before.

It does not matter what has happened in your past. The past is behind you. The past can be an anchor and chain around your neck or it can be the fuel that propels you forward. In the past I let others define me and I let events control me. True success happened when I decided that I am the only one who can define me.

> *No one will deny me and nobody will define me*
> *I am the only one who will decide who I am*
> *I am the only who will decide who I will become.*
> *My belief in who I am will power my mind*
> *My actions will revolutionize my world.*
> *... because I am a Superstar.*
>
> — Excerpt from *I am a Superstar* by Croix Sather

Get inspired by my video *I AM A SUPERSTAR*. It is my gift to you. Use it, adapt it, remember and internalize it. This creed is what I use on my long runs to keep me going for hours after my body says "Enough!" I share it with my seminar audiences and it always gets them fired up. Whenever I need to get out of a funk, I use this creed to bring me back up to superstar energy. When everything is going my way, I declare this creed to reinforce who I am and the purpose of my life. *See the video at: www.DreamBigActBig.com/champion*

It wasn't always the case that I knew I was the only one who could define me. I didn't know it at the time because my parents protected me from many of the harsh realities in the world. My parents had just moved out of a Brooklyn neighborhood where crime was becoming an epidemic. I was born just after they escaped the cement jungle. We moved in a decent apartment in the suburbs of New York City giving us a safe place to grow up and play.

My dad was a young man and the idea of being around chirping crickets and a town that went to sleep at six o'clock was not what he thought it would be. In the beginning he would pace on the back porch at night. Like a caged tiger he would walk nine feet to the railing and then turn around and go back. He worked as a carpenter building houses for a boss with no mercy. Each night he would come home dead tired from framing homes.

The tiger got used to his new home and he would snooze on the couch from exhaustion after dinner. He would then get up, tuck us in bed and go to sleep, only to start the same routine over again the next day. He busted his back six days a week when the work was available. This is a work ethic that I would inherit. When the work was slow and money was tight my parents would go to sleep without eating so that my brothers and I would have dinner. Swinging a hammer was over on Saturday, but there was more work to be done. On Sundays we would drive to Manhattan where he was a preacher for a small congregation. I don't know when he found the time to write and prepare his sermons, but he always found a way to make it happen.

Like most mothers of the seventies, my mom was a stay-at-home mom. She was as dedicated as they come. Mom woke before dawn and breakfast was waiting for us when we came into the kitchen. Dinner was ready for us when dad got home and we were expected to come in from play to be ready for dinner by 5:30. Mom was nurturing and tough. The Brooklyn attitude and accent wouldn't fade for decades. It is one of the greatest gifts I ever received. Today I raise my children with a similar style because I see what happens to children when the parents are pushovers and obedient to the child's demands. Being a parent is the most challenging duty one can ever have. Also the most important and rewarding.

Mom also raised us to be tough and resilient. It is probably what saved my life on several occasions. My dad was typically quiet when it came to how we were raised. If my mom ever had to follow through on the phrase, "Do you want me to get your father?" there was hell to pay. Despite his size and his occasional rule enforcing, my dad was actually a teddy bear. He was and still is all heart. My dad always made each one of use feel special and important. He always made one-on-one time for us. I can remember that *my* time was when he first got home. He would pick me up and hug me and spend a few minutes with me before he got cleaned up for dinner. Every once in a while he would bring me home a matchbox car that I would play with for hours and hours in the back yard. Later on as I grew he would bring me out for breakfast on Saturday mornings when he wasn't working.

When I was seven years old we moved one block down the road to our first house. I learned that owning your own home is one of the greatest joys of your life. Only a couple of years later my dad would quit his job and start his own business. His brother who had been a builder for many years gave him one of his old vans with "Sather Construction" already labeled on the side. I remember my dad saying many times over the years, "My worst year in business for myself was better than my best year working for my old boss." This obviously became embedded in my subconscious because I have almost always run my own business. Not all of them have been successful, but I have almost always cut my own path.

By the time I finished physical rehabilitation after the drunk driver hit me on my bicycle when I was fourteen, I had lost my desire to compete as a swimmer. When I lost the only identity I was proud of, my life became a rollercoaster of success and failure. I would achieve some success – sometimes extraordinary success – and then sabotage those successes, bringing me back to the starting block. Looking back now I know that my self-sabotage was to bring me back to a place where I was comfortable. Most often comfortable meant living by someone else's definitions and beliefs of life.

How We Are Defined

It may seem like we are self-made. It may seem like we are who we are because of our innate personalities. This is only partially true. We are in a very large part designed by our environment. As a child we are shaped by those who raised us, taught us, by the events that we experienced and the environments in which we grew up. This is unique even for siblings, because others treat you differently. You react to these stimuli in part because of your inborn design and in part because of how you have seen others react. It is what you have seen, learned and experienced that plays a major role in who you are today.

For many, that never changes. Few people break free from those influences. They live by other's rules and limiting beliefs. Those teachings and those events that shaped your life may have served you in the past, but many of your behaviors do not serve you today. Some of the lessons you learned become out of date and ineffective as you grow older, while other programming will always serve you – like my mother instilling the importance of resiliency and my father illustrating the value of entrepreneurialism.

When I was doing my training in hypnotherapy we watched the teacher work with a volunteer student, a fifty-something divorced man. When he was regressed back to his childhood it became clear why he was stuck in life. As a child he was sitting on a chair in the kitchen and he was in trouble. His mom had just berated him because of what happened a few minutes before when he was outside. There was a line of bushes in the front yard dividing the yard from the busy road. He had gone to the other side of those bushes, outside of the boundaries that his mother had dictated to him. Of course her punishment was done out of love. His mom wanted to keep him safe and protect him from the traffic. What he learned and held onto for his whole life was the belief that he must stay in the boundaries or you lose love. He was now at a job working for a major company that he hated but he could not leave. His life program was still that of the little boy. Leaving the company would be going out of the boundaries of what is expected of him. It is no longer his mom; now it's his peers, his boss, and society that determine those boundaries for him.

Whenever I would achieve success that was out of my comfort zone, I would find a way to screw it up and sabotage myself. At twenty-four I bought my first house. It was a four-thousand-square-foot Federal-style Victorian that I bought for pennies on the dollar. It looked similar to the White House with the big white columns. It was a dilapidated mess that should have been condemned, but it was still amazing. My wife and I had been married three years already when I proudly said, "I found us a home!" When I showed her the house she hated it. She wanted something small and simple. She also wanted a house that had heat, water and windows. This house had none of those things.

I spent three years rebuilding that house into its previous glory. I admit it was not a fun adventure for her. The house went through major restructuring. At times there were ladders to get to the bedroom and there was always dust and debris. I didn't mind the process – it was exciting to me – but it was not something she could appreciate. Business suits and a construction zone were not a good combination in her eyes.

Before the house was finished, our marriage was. I realized years later that I had ignored the person who should have been the most important person in my life. Everything and everyone else came before her. Of course it wasn't intentional to ignore my marriage, it just happened because I was immature and unaware of the *important* things in life. Loving someone and showing your love are two very different things. We both agreed that being with each other was not a good combination. We wanted very different things and had very different values systems so I finished the house. Then we sold it and went our separate ways.

I was raised in a traditional home. When you married, you stayed married no matter what. Getting a divorce haunted me for years. I let it define me as a failure. Now I was one of *those* people who had an X and I was still in my twenties. It made me *feel* like damaged goods haunting me for years.

As time went on and I became a little wiser I started to observe successful marriages, failed marriages where people stayed together anyway, and people who got divorced. Successful marriages always have the same formula. The couple has similar core values and they make the other person feel like the most important person in the world. Failed marriages were always the reverse – they had different core values and treated the other person in a mediocre to poor fashion. Sometimes they were down right nasty. These couples stay together because the familiarity was less painful than the perceived pain of change. Divorced couples were typically people who simply got tired of the situation where the relationship caused enough pain to incite divorce.

What does this have to do with becoming a superstar and rising to your full potential? Everything! Life is about the experience. Your relationships are the biggest component of your experiences. If your most intimate relationships are glorious and strong, your whole life is the same, and when you are thrown a speed bump it is so much easier to deal with. If your most important and intimate relationships are in turmoil, your ability to excel will be limited. There are no stronger emotions that will make you do stupid things than when you are falling *in* love or falling *out* of love.

I learned that relationships work when the core values are in alignment and they fail miserably when they are not. This is true for personal relationships as well as family, friends and business. A core value is the most important value that a person lives by. All values are important in a person's life, but it is the order and magnitude of certainty, significance, uncertainty, love, and connectedness that determine how a person will behave. If one person likes structure and organization and the other person is spontaneous, it is likely to be a challenge. It's fun in the beginning, but long term, not so much. Take that same couple and the spontaneous person has a high libido and the structured one does not, that relationship is destine for friction. Not the kind the spontaneous person wants. If you are positive and outgoing and your spouse is quiet, shy and a pessimist, you are headed for internal and emotional conflict.

They say that opposites attract, but that is not the case when it comes to core values. The one or two highest priority needs and values determine how you live your life. In other words, where your center of gravity is. If one person is active in sports and the other is not, then one person always feels left out or self-conscious. If one is social and the other is not, the social one always feels like the other is a wet blanket and the non-social one feels like the other should stay home more.

Eventually what was once endearing becomes nauseating.

Core operating values will affect friendships, family, business relationships, and even sales. This has nothing to do with the other person being good or bad, it is about being different, having different emotional programs, and wanting different things. In business it may be advantageous to hire or work with an opposite if you know and understand that you are different at your core. You can use each other's strengths to get further than you would on your own or with another person aligned with you.

When we are no longer able to change a situation, we are challenged to change ourselves. – Viktor Frankl, Holocaust survivor and author of Man's Search For Meaning.

When someone does something differently than you do, instead of judging them ask yourself, "Why are they doing that?" If you can understand their values or programs that influence their decisions, you can be a better friend, lover, boss, parent or leader.

Determining and Breaking Through Self-Sabotage

Self-sabotage or self-defeating behaviors happen to everyone. It is a part of being human, so stop expecting perfection and strive to always get better. Self-defeating and self-sabotaging behavior includes procrastination, indecision, anger, lack of focus, chemical addiction, self-pity, self-doubt, and many more.

Self-defeating behavior is easy to find. These are the things that you do on a regular basis that you know are bad but you do them anyway. You have a report due by Friday and you wait until the last minute and then have to stop everything to rush to get it done. You leave the dishes in the sink even though you know it angers your spouse. You don't return important phone calls.

These all occur due to an underlying cause. If you are not returning important phone calls it may be because you lack confidence in yourself, your ability, or your production. Or you may hate your job and it is your way of making the moment easier. Both are making your life more difficult in the long term. You are paying for it in reduced income, lower self-worth, unfulfilling relationships, and emotional turmoil.

To break through you must first recognize the pattern. I try to do this myself. When I have an emotional block to getting things done, my pattern is to find trivial or nonessential things to do. The project may be due tomorrow, but my self-doubt shows up as snacking, tidying up, answering emails, and organizing. These are all called *non-confronts*. You find other things so you have a fabricated "excuse" not to do what is important. "I was too busy to get it done." You're full of fertilizer. You procrastinated. We all do it. Successful people find a way to get focused and stay on what is important.

What are your non-confronts? When you recognize one happening you have to stop. What do you do instead of doing what you need to do? Think about why you are doing it. Are you afraid of rejection or failure? Whatever the reason is you must find an empowering reason to move forward and do what a successful person does. Is your reason your family? Your purpose? Or is it pride of accomplishment? What are the consequences if you keep screwing around and ignore what's important? Will you feel like a loser when you have wasted your precious time? Will your income suffer and it will be another year of just scraping by?

Recognize your patterns, reframe, and adjust to make progress.

Self-sabotaging behavior can be unconscious and more difficult to determine. Take Joe, a regular guy with a regular salaried job. He gets an unexpected $5,000 bonus. He's excited and starts thinking about what he can buy with his newfound wealth. Before the check is cashed he buys an entertainment center with a fifty-inch plasma television that he has been eyeing in the electronics catalogue. When he tells his wife, she reminds him about more than $7,000 in credit card debt and the new roof they need and the fact that they have no savings. Instead cancelling the television order, he justifies it by saying he will work overtime for that other stuff. But the overtime never seems to happen.

Joe's financial pattern is to spend more than he has. It's his pattern to think about the instant gratification rather than the deeper and more beneficial benefit. He probably learned it by observing his parents or another authority in his childhood. The more money that comes in, the more it goes out. When the money slows, it still goes out just as fast. A better solution would have been to pay off the high interest credit card debt and go out to dinner to celebrate your fabulous decision. The bonus check could have been a get-out-of-jail-free card that would have eliminated most of his debt and saving hundreds a month in interest payments.

Recognize your patterns, reframe, and adjust to make progress.

Center of Gravity

In your home there is a thermostat set to a certain temperature. If you have it set on seventy degrees and it gets a few degrees too cold the thermostat sends a signal to the furnace and the heat comes on. When the room temperature reaches seventy the thermostat stops sending the signal to the furnace and it stops producing heat. When it gets too hot the thermostat sends a signal to the air conditioner and it cools down the house.

You have a thermostat for each of your values just like the thermostat in your home.

Nobody can stay on a perfect diet, play a perfect game, or lead a perfect life. But that is what many people expect of themselves. Then when something does not go perfectly, they beat themselves up. When someone has the programming to be "at a certain temperature" she will sabotage her efforts to stay in her comfort zone.

Diets don't work for this reason. Most diets expect you to eat specific meals in specific quantities and never vary. It is too restrictive and sometimes even sadistic.

Those who lose weight and keep it off are the people who change their center of gravity. In other words, they reset the thermostat to a new number. Some call this a *set point*. A diet is like opening the window in winter. It may cool off the room for a while, but once you close the window the room goes back to its original temperature. Or in this case a person's original weight. You are asking your body and your emotions to keep you some place they are very unfamiliar with.

You can also see this law in action with people who win the lottery. With in a few years of winning millions many lottery winners are bankrupt. The reason – they never reset their financial thermostat. If you have an overspending habit when you are making fifty thousand a year (like Joe buying the plasma TV), winning lotto is only going to amplify that habit. It will also happen to a lotto winner who is uncomfortable with money. That person will give it all away because the emotion of having that much money is too great of a burden for that person. Some people have a financial thermostat of zero and others it is set for a negative number. The minority have a financial blueprint that is set for saving or earning more money than is spent.

Your center of gravity is the same as your physical center of gravity. If you are knocked off balance while you are walking, you correct yourself to stay standing upright. Just like a boat wants to always right itself. Think of someone who is always grumpy and complaining. There are plenty of those. Now think of someone who is always happy and positive. The grumpy person has a center of gravity down in the grumpy zone, while a positive person has their center of gravity up in the happy zone. This doesn't mean that the happy person is always happy, but that is where they are most of the time. Like the thermostat, there is a certain amount of variation and it always moves back to the set point. You have the ability to change your center of gravity for attitude, happiness, gratitude, work ethic or any thing else.

What Determines a Center of Gravity?

When a person grows up in an environment where the people are always finding fault in others and complaining, it will likely set their thermostat for that kind of attitude. The same goes for financial set points and health set points. If you want to change your set point you may need to change your environment or the way people behave around you by setting up parameters. "Hey guys, I love you, but when you complain it brings me down. Let's keep it light and upbeat – Okay?"

You can watch trash TV like Jerry Springer that fills your head with garbage, or you can turn off the tube and read more books like this one that teaches you have grow. Both will help set your center of gravity. My environment is always filled with positive people and my car always has an audiobook playing or music that charges me. If I end up in a situation that is dark or heavy, I leave or adjust the attitude.

As we covered in the chapter *What You Focus on Expands,* your center of gravity is also determined by what you focus on. This is why I have audio books in my car, it is why I watch movies and talks (see TED.com) that inspire me, and why my core social circle is intensely positive. It is also why I continually go back to training and seminars. I need my fix of possibility and motivation. As motivational legend Zig Ziglar said in his distinctly southern accent, "Motivation is like a shower. You can go without it, but I wouldn't recommend it."

You are the gatekeeper of your mind. Your environment and the information you expose yourself to will determine the outcome of your life. When I was in my late teens and early twenties I started listening to personal development tapes. You know, cassette tapes? Those things before CDs and iPods. When others heard what I was listening to I was teased and mocked. After a while of this, I became a closet self-help follower. When I started growing as a person and become more positive, I was once again teased. "You listening to those tapes again? Why do you bother? It's not going to change anything." To keep from losing friends and love, I stopped listening. Many years later I realized that those people who were ridiculing me were broke and unhappy. If I do what they tell me then I will always stay at that level. Broke and unhappy doesn't work for me? How 'bout you?

If you want to change your center of gravity, if you want to change the number on your thermostat, surround yourself with those people who have achieved what you want to achieve. Surround yourself with people who have the lifestyle that you want to have. Get yourself into the social circles of people doing what you want to do. Learn everything you can about what you dream about. You can become happier by learning the strategies of happiness. If you want to be wealthy, study wealthy people. Get your information from many sources and then synthesize all of that information and act upon it. It all comes back to action. You have to take action to be around certain people and to get certain information and then you have to act to become that person you dream about.

But this is not about social climbing. It's not about mortgaging your house to pay for admission to the country club. It's not about being phony or putting on airs. It's about striving to be your best and to place yourself only in those environments where success and excellence are valued.

Changing your center of gravity is also recognizing when you are moving away from where you want to be. *Change that pattern and get back on track.*

For instance, one of my clients was always late. He was late because he has a lousy sense of time. But when he realized he had a problem, he had enough self-awareness to make a correction. Now he sets his alarm for ten minutes earlier than he must leave. This gives him enough time to finish an email, pack his laptop, hit the bathroom and get out the door. If he does not do this, he knows he will be late because he will work too long and then he is stressed and rushed and looks very unprofessional.

CLIMB YOUR MOUNTAIN

Except for the few mountains that rise out of the desert's uniformity, the land just outside Phoenix, Arizona is flat as far as your eye can see. I arrived early to attend a speaker's boot camp with World Champion Speakers Darren LaCroix, Craig Valentine, and Ed Tate. I always arrive a day early for my events and plan a free day to do something fun. On this trip I decided to go for a run. This was long before I ran regularly. But there was something about the desert that called to me.

As you drive to the mountains they erupt from the arid plains. I drove into the state park and chose the tallest mountain. From the base to the peak of Camelback Mountain it is about thirteen hundred vertical feet of climb. Instead of the direct route, I chose the trail that goes around the mountain for a five-mile loop and then up to the peak. Not knowing what I was in for I thought, "It's only five miles."

I grabbed one bottle of water and headed off. I started with a jog running up the ragged and gnarly trail. I only made it a half-mile before I was panting and bent over in exhaustion from the heat. It was seven in the morning and it was already ninety-one degrees in the shade. As I hid in the shade of an eight-foot cactus, I took a sip of water and continued on, this time walking.

As I neared the first ridge going around the mountain I passed another hiker coming the opposite direction. He was decked out in the latest hiking gear. He looked like an ad for a mountain climbing company complete with large brimmed hat, a water backpack, and carbon fiber hiking poles. I thought, "Come on, this is only five miles – you don't need all that stuff." Then I passed a couple more hikers like that. It was getting hotter, sweat was pouring off me, and I was down to a half-bottle of water and now I am thinking, maybe they are on to something.

The trail climbs around the backside of the mountain heading back down towards the flat desert. Somewhere on the backside of the mountain, you reach a sign post that says "Freedom Trail." The sign was telling the truth. We are free. Free to go create a life by our design, a life that makes us happy. Or we are free to remain unchanged and accept what we already have and what has come our way by chance.

I was in a transition in my life. Going from a world that was familiar and comfortable to a world that was unfamiliar and uncertain. Down to a few ounces in my water bottle, I knew that I didn't have enough water for the journey. I wasn't sure if I was even at the halfway point yet or not. If I went back, at least I knew what it would be like. I knew how far and the level of difficulty. When you are uncertain of what is ahead, it 's easy to go back to the familiar.

Continuing on I walked into the shade created by the mountain in the low morning sun. The cooler temperature of the shade was very welcome. The hike became comfortable for the moment as I started to ascend. As I climbed higher, I climbed back into the sun and closing in on the end of the loop. I found that I had already completed the majority of the trail with only the climb to the peak to go.

It can be intimidating to go forward on a path that you have never been on. Had I turned around when I saw the marker, it would have been further and more difficult to return than continuing forward. Plus I would have missed the climb to the peak. I took my last sip of water, and headed onward and upward to the peak.

I made it to the end of the trail and the view was incredible in one direction. But the very top of the mountain was still a little higher and blocked some of the view. I turned to the sign that said, "No one beyond this point" and smiled as I hurdled the rail and climbed above the trail to the very peak, where I sat down at the pinnacle. It's an amazing view from the top of Camelback Mountain. You can see three-hundred-sixty degrees. You can see Phoenix off in the distance and the desert seems to go forever. It is a truly spectacular view.

How many times have you been so close to a big accomplishment but you quit because it still seemed so far away, only later to discover that you had almost made it?

Even though the trail and climb were small by most measures, the lessons are invaluable.

1 **You are further along than it seems**

2 **You are closer to the goal than it feels**

3 **Go prepared**

4 **The journey seems most difficult and lonely just before the end**

5 **The view from the very top is amazing**

6 **Climb one mountain at a time.**

Let me explain number six, *climb one mountain at a time*. This is a lesson that many never learn, especially entrepreneurial and creative types. It is a lesson that evaded me up until I sat on top of that mountain.

Many people spend their life bouncing from one idea to the next, or one job to the next, or one relationship to the next. Never staying in one place for long enough to become extraordinary. There are many things that you can do to become a superstar if you just choose *one* great idea and *stick to it*.

FINDING YOUR **ONE** MOUNTAIN

Many people ask me after one of my seminars, "How do I find my true purpose in life?" They then the person will tell me about all of the different thing he is dabbling in. It is the same question I asked myself for years. Tough question, maybe the toughest you will ever ask, if you ask it that way.

What if you asked a different question? Instead ask, "What is my next purpose in life?"

Many times we think we must find the one true purpose for our existence in life. There's a common fairly tale that we are meant to grow up and fulfill one role from birth and that even as a young child we should know what this is. This is occasionally true. Were you born a prince or a princess? Where you a prodigy at age four? If you are not one of these or something similar, then your life is as much about what you make of it, as much as it is about serendipity.

Many of my clients come to me trying to figure this out. Confused and discouraged, they want to give up. Instead, they find a coach that can help. Winners never quit. When faced with an obstacle, superstars try something different until they get the result they want.

The challenge is in the belief that you have only one true purpose that you must find to be complete. What if you have different purposes for different stages in your life? What if your purpose cannot be revealed until you first accomplish something else? Sometimes there is a barrier to entry. Often what a person does now opens the door to the next and even bigger purpose, but most never get there because they did not make any significant progress in any one area. People who make a major impact in the world often work in one career for five or ten or more years, and then they leap to another because an opportunity arose out that experience. It is not about *one* purpose, but what is your purpose *now*?

How can you have an impact now?

Many superstars were heading in a different direction earlier in their career. Then something happened. Because they were extraordinary at what they did, they were recognized and offered jobs, opportunities and partnerships that they never planned, bringing them down a very different road. David Letterman was a weatherman and a writer for the sitcom *Good Times*, Angelina Jolie wanted to be a funeral director before she got some small roles in music videos, Marlon Brando was a gravedigger after being kicked out of military school, and Garth Brooks sold boots right up until his big break.

Life has an amazing way of helping you when you are moving in a forward direction with zeal and passion. Most stars never would have been given the opportunity if they hadn't been out there hustling to make something happen.

Action Item

Step 1:

To find your next purpose, make three vertical columns on a sheet of paper. Now take ten minutes with inspirational background music playing and fill in the columns:

Column 1 - List of everything you would like to do "LIKES"

Column 2 – List of everything you are good or great at "STRENGTHS"

Column 3 – List of things you love to do (hobbies, work, everything) "PASSIONS"

Fill in the three columns with everything you can think of. Do not filter your ideas – write down everything. This is a worksheet not the Declaration of Independence and you can always add more later.

Step 2:

On a clean sheet of paper write your resume and bio in short bullet form. This is called "ABOUT ME." Write down everything you have ever done. Both the noteworthy and not so noteworthy. This is also a draft for brainstorming ideas, not to pass out for employment. Write down jobs you've held, volunteering, hobbies, adventures, and anything else that you have ever done or been a part of.

Step 3:

On another sheet of paper, write down all of your personal accomplishments, abilities and activities that you have ever done. This is called "FUN & FAB." Write down vacations, likes, goals reached.

Step 4:

This is another fun page called "POSSIBILITIES." Take another clean sheet of paper and write down all of the things you would like to do, be and experience. These can be family, career, volunteer, spiritual, and vacation related. Anything that you have ever dreamed of doing, seeing or being a part of. This doesn't mean that you will do it. It is simply a collection of ideas and possibilities of things you may do.

Step 5:

Now take those papers and read what you wrote. What jumps out at you, where are there parallels, and what sounds cool? Writing it out helps your mind process differently and helps you see patterns.

In this step you will start a mind map. Google "mind map" if you are not familiar with this idea. It's an easy concept and an online search will get you examples as well as instructions.

In the center draw a bubble and write the word that best describes what you want to accomplish or find an answer. Examples are: Dream Career, The Next Adventure, or My Purpose.

From there you will make six lines away from the center bubble in different directions and write in the corresponding bubbles "Likes," "Strengths," "Passions," "About Me," "Fun & Fab," and "Possibilities."

Now take your worksheets and start filling in around the bubbles. This mind-mapping style allows for a non-linear way of thinking. I made several of these when planning my Run Across America and I make them for many other reasons. What I like most about mind maps is that it is fun and allows me to capture ideas in a way more like the way my brain works.

Post your mind map to a wall or on an easel. What do you see? Do you see patterns of your interests? Are there things about your personality that didn't see before? You may see a career path that you never considered before or see something that you are particularly suited for. Does something give you additional ideas? Fill in the new ideas. As you look and think about what your next step in life is, start filling in around the bubble called "Possibilities." Don't edit, just write. All of your ideas are great. The only dumb thing you can do is NOT write an idea down. One idea may be silly, but it may trigger a new spectacular idea. Allow your mind to wander and imagine what could be as you create your mind map. As Albert Einstein once said, "Imagination is more important than knowledge."

Did you find your next adventure? After just thirty minutes or so, you may find some amazing insights that you didn't know about yourself. Do some research on your main ideas then take action on the one idea that is most appealing and create your future. If nothing jumps out at you today, that's okay. Your subconscious mind will keep working on it even after you stop. Come back each day and spend a few minutes with this mind map. And if you are still stuck go ask your friends for advice. Show them your mind map and ask, "What do you think I would be amazing at?" Or find a great life or career coach to help guide you.

As you go through this process always think about how you can help others or support a cause. How can you make an impact on the world? You will find passion and purpose in serving others. This may mean you become an amazing singer or artist and your "work" will inspire others. You may directly serve others as a counselor or participant in an event. You may also help others by working on a project for a company that you are passionate about, such as the animators who work on Pixar movies and designers who create the next generation of cars or technology. Your possibilities are endless. As motivational pioneer Zig Ziglar said, "Help enough people get what they want and you will get what you want."

For some people there may be too many opportunities. Some people are very good at many things and they could have excellent careers in many fields. And yet, they accomplish little because they cannot decide their purpose. Will you be a rock star, CEO, real estate mogul, Broadway dancer, actor, magician, American president, leader of a cause, find the cure for cancer, or bring water to rural Africa? The possibilities are endless and all are achievable.

It all goes back to – What is next? Pick one thing and be the best you can in it. You will either become amazing at it and stay there or it will launch you into the next phase of your life. Whatever you do, do something. Stop procrastinating and *do something*.

Make life happen. The world needs you.

WHAT ALL SUPERSTARS DO

All superstars have one quality in common. You won't read many articles about it. You won't see it in interviews and you won't read many articles about it or hear many people talking about it because its not Hollywood or glamorous. At least not to most people. It's incredibly glamorous and even sort of sexy to those who lead an incredible life of adventure because they know it is one of the most important and common attributes in superstars and icons.

Imagine that every year of your life you got better. Every year you became smarter and every year you were always on top of your game. How amazing would life be if you were always improving?

The Japanese business culture calls this *Kaizen*. It means constant and never-ending improvement and change for the better. Japanese businesses aim for small and incremental steps as a means of making incredible products. Here is the magical part. In the process of small and incremental change, each new improvement builds on past improvement and it begins to amplify all previous improvements. Plus, some significant leaps occur as a result of constant and never ending improvement.

In my seminars, I teach a version of this called *One Degree of Change*. If you do not improve your life, by default you will regress. For example, physical fitness. If you do not exercise and strengthen your muscles, your muscles will atrophy and get weaker and your health will deteriorate. This is the same for relationships, career, and emotional fortitude.

If you are not growing you are dying.

One degree of change means improving one thing just a little bit. An increment of one degree of improvement may not mean much in the moment, but over time it grows and grows making for massive amounts of change. Then add another degree of change on top of that previous change and stretch that out over time and it becomes more than double the results. Keep adding regular change and improvement and soon you are living the life of your dreams and it took seemingly little effort because it was a lot of little steps of growth.

Kaizen and one degree of change must be a daily ritual in your life. When it is, your life becomes better and better. Soon your life becomes great, then it is extraordinary, and your life still continues gets better. This applies to your health, relationships, career, emotions, psychology, and spiritual life. When one aspect of your life improves other parts will improve with it. As John F. Kennedy stated, "A rising tide lifts all boats."

TEN STRATEGIES TO BECOMING A SUPERSTAR

These strategies apply to becoming a superstar as well as being noticed as a superstar. Unleash the Superstar Within and then get noticed for your amazing abilities and efforts. There are good ways to get noticed and there are great ways to get noticed. One of these ideas alone will get you noticed. Combine several and you are certain to garner well-deserved attention.

1 Go Big!

Go really freakin' big. This is the first part of the formula because it gets you noticed as a star quickly and you get noticed for doing something awesome. Think I ran across the country only because I want to go sightseeing? My Run Across America is to spread a needed message, to prove anything is possible, to inspire young adults to rise above and Break Through and Unleash the Superstar Within. It is also to live what I teach. What kind of coach would I be if I told what to do, if I wasn't doing it myself? In the process of doing something extraordinary, and helping thousands of people in the process, the run is also designed to bring me national and global recognition.

Go big in a way that seems impossible. So big that everyone thinks you are crazy. Disney World, The Panama Canal, hot-air ballooning around the world, Google, getting on the *New York Times* best seller list, and building a casino in the desert are all examples of going really big.

If you are not hitting resistance you're thinking too small. Spectators must be in awe with the idea and think you are not playing with a full deck. You should hear questions like, "Is that possible? Has anyone ever done that before? Why hasn't anyone ever done it before? Can you die doing that?" Don't worry about telling others or someone stealing your idea. If it is big enough, nobody will want to attempt it. I didn't have a single person ask to run thirty miles a day with me and run across America. At moments I wondered if the goal was too big. At times I wondered if it was possible for me. You want your idea to be so grand that you don't have any competition.

2   Be Infectious With Enthusiasm

You got this great idea and now you have to sell it. If you are certain that your idea has the power to change your life, the lives of others and have a positively impact, then the only people you have to sell are yourself and those who are helping you make it happen. Your spouse, friend, family and the rest of the world will become fans once they see it happening.

The easiest way to get people excited about your idea is to be excited and enthusiastic yourself. This is a no-brainer, but is often overlooked because most people are shy about being excited. You must be so enthusiastic it is contagious. Just like a child wanting to go to Disney World, you must be as excited and persistent as a five-year-old. Enthusiasm opens doors that would otherwise be dead bolted. When you are electrified with passion for your idea or product, people will want to be a part of your team and help you succeed even if they are uncertain how you will make it happen. And those who are not moved or excited by your ideas are not right for your team or vision. It is a process of self-elimination.

When your enthusiasm is intoxicating, people will notice you. Others will talk about you and spread the word. Connectors will introduce you to others who can help you or will want to be a part of your adventure. True enthusiasm works because it speaks from your heart and soul with authenticity.

3 Boldness Is Rewarded and How I had Lunch with John Assaraf

Have you ever wondered why some people seem to always be with the cool crowd? Ever wonder why some people are at the best events and rubbing shoulders with the stars? Sometimes it is whom you know. Most often it is up to you.

A great friend of mine was traveling from Los Angeles to Orlando. On the plane there was a buzz –"Patrick Dempsey is on the plane," she heard people whispering. Katie said to herself, "If I don't ask, I don't get." She walked up from economy to first class, squatted down in front of the dreamy doc, and said, "Hi, I'm Katie Joy. I'm from Australia." She paused to let him take it in. "Can I take a photo with you?" The man in the next seat took the camera from her hands as she sat in Patrick's lap for the moment to be immortalized. "Thank you. You made my day." Katie said as she left him in peace for the rest of the trip.

Not a single other person on the plane asked for a photo. Not even after Katie did it first. Only Katie got the photo op with McDreamy because she overcame the fear of possible rejection or embarrassment and she asked for what she wanted. How many times had you wished that you acted like Katie? How many times did you miss the opportunity to get a photo, go on a trip, take a job, or start a relationship?

I was at a conference to learn from Internet marketing genius Frank Kern. I didn't realize how many stars were at this event. It was a who's–who of several industries. At the lunch break I was walking out alone and heard someone in front of me say, "Let's go to that Thai restaurant we ate at last night. It was amazing."

I love Thai food. So I asked, "Can I join you?" Nobody said no, so I took that as a yes. I followed them for four blocks. As we were walking there I realized whom I was walking with. It was John Assaraf from the movie and book *The Secret*, Brendon Burchard, author of *Life's Golden Ticket* and founder of *Experts Academy*, and other millionaire superstars with their entourage. It was a fabulous lunch and conversation that made connections for me that only happened because I took bold action and invited myself to lunch. Was some of it good luck? Certainly, but without taking bold action it was nothing. At lunch I connected with some of the group. Later that night I was invited by one of the superstars to a private party and rubbed elbows with more superstars.

Boldness gets you noticed. Boldness gets you goodies that others wish they had. Asking and taking action gets you into events that are otherwise invitation only. Boldness keeps you moving toward your dream. Don't stop and think, "What if he says no? What if I embarrass myself? What if I fail? What if they don't like me?" Stop being a wuss. Stop projecting what others may or may not do and go ask for what you want. Sometimes it is not going to work. When it does work it gets photos with stars, dinner with icons, and friendships or business connections with amazing people. Business is done this way and opportunities manifest. Who knows, maybe you will even find the love of your life.

4   Be Amazing

It is easy to get noticed if you are Michael Phelps, Venus Williams, Patricia Cornwell, Garth Brooks, or the winner of *America's Got Talent*. You can also get noticed by being infamous. How else do you explain Paris? The person, not the city. Here's the thing – superstars are rarely one-hit-wonders. They are amazing through and through. They are not necessarily the best, but they are extraordinary. And they are persistent in getting noticed for their talents. Even Paris.

You have to excel in what you do to get noticed and become a superstar. Often icons are great at what they do, but they are not the best. You have to be great, extraordinary, or amazing to stand out, *but you do not have to be the best in the world.* If you are a quarterback for any professional football team, you are extraordinary. You don't get there if you are mediocre. I have crossed paths with many professional speakers who have average skills on the stage. And yet, they are making a fabulous income and traveling the world doing what they love, which is speaking to audiences. They usually have great information or they are entertaining and often both, but their technical skills are lame.

This is important to you because you must understand that you do not have to be the best to be a superstar. I see it all the time. Very talented people who are paralyzed from creating the life they talk about and want because they are *perfectionists*. They also have this stupid self-limiting belief (like I once did) that they have to be perfect to be hired. So they don't bother applying for the job, or sending out their one-sheets, or demo videos, or any marketing material.

This doesn't mean that you can be horrible and expect to get hired. The best way to getting hired, getting a gig, or being hired by a client is to astound them. You must stand out and be amazing. How do you get amazing? Do what you love and dedicate yourself to the craft. Find and learn skills that make you unique and special. What's more impressive – a juggler with tennis balls or a juggler with flaming knives? The latter one is cool. But what if you juggled flaming knives from a tightrope 2,000 feet in the air on a unicycle? This is why someone like David Blaine stands out. He does extraordinary street magic that is unusual and captivating so much more than your typical magic.

Just as importantly, you have to be *personable*. It is so much more than just about skill. This is a key part of being amazing. I am regularly told that I have an incredible ability to connect with people and to make them feel comfortable and inspired. This is more important than almost anything else I do. I can be in front of an audience of one or one thousand and I can connect with you at a visceral level. This is partially an effect of my environment, part innate, but most importantly it is my dedication to connecting with others. I built on what was already there and took ownership of it.

You have unique and innate talents to build on too. Don't deny them.

David Blaine is recognized for his larger-than-life performances. He has well-developed charisma and an unusual style. This must certainly be intentional. He gets you emotionally charged and excited. He stands out as one of the best in the world because of his personality as well as his techniques.

Oprah is amazing because she is as lovable as she is a relentless entrepreneur. She stands out for going above and beyond what any other talk show has done. Oprah is adored not just for her huge promotions and giveaways; she is adored because she still represents the everyday person. She is the voice of her followers and they love her for that.

There are many very talented people that we never hear about. Why? Because the world doesn't know about them. They are conservative, boring, and mediocre. They may be talented, they may even be the best in the world, but if they don't find a way to let the world know, then they remain undiscovered. If they do not find a way to connect with an audience, they remain a mystery. When you connect your talent with a charismatic personality you become amazing and you stand out. You will be noticed and you will go places.

5   Be Outrageous

Howard Stern, Jerry Springer, Jim Carrey, Matthew Lesko, Richard Branson's hot air balloon flights around the world, and David Blaine escaping from a block of frozen ice in Times Square. Rude, crazy, funny, or sensational, they get attention because they stand out. Way out.

Ask yourself what is going to get national or even global media coverage? What is going to spread virally on the web? Rule out the illegal and immoral stuff and then find something great to further your position as an expert or further your cause. Publicity stunts sometimes work, but they are usually short lived. I am talking about real and useful events that get you noticed as a superstar in your area of expertise. Even better, something that is bigger than you and will help others.

The *Free Hugs* campaign started out as a simple idea that got worldwide attention for spreading love with the simple act of a hug. Doesn't seem all that outrageous to give hugs in the city center, and yet it was bold enough, and out-of-the-box enough to get global awareness making hugs more accepted. I love hugs, don't you? Hug You!

The Blair Witch Project is a movie based on the story of three film students who went missing while investigating and interviewing people about the legend of Blair Witch in a town once called Blair, Maryland. A year later the film and audio footage were found in a cabin bringing the story into the public spotlight. It was a fabulous execution of story, publicity, and carefully crafted hype tugging on the panic strings of your darkest fears. The story, of course, was completely fabricated. It was a low-budget film that cost a paltry $22,000 and grossed almost $250 million in worldwide release.

6   Be Relentless

Superstars are relentless in the pursuit of making their dreams come true. This is why you must LOVE, LOVE, LOVE what you do. You are the heart and soul of your project, campaign, and product. If you don't believe in it, who will? If you are not relentless in your pursuit of your dream, why should the people whom you hire be relentless?

This does not mean "hard work." Why? It's not work at all, because you would do it for *free*. That is what it means to follow your passion in life. Your work and your results are a labor of love. Confucius said, "Choose a job you love and you will never have to work a day in your life." Your work and your passion should be the same. When they are the same, it is easy to get past the rejections, the challenges and what Seth Godin calls "the dip." Pushing through the difficult part of starting a new business or endeavor. Loving what I do is what will keep me running thirty miles every day for one hundred days and giving a free keynote seminar and taking on the financial risks of making it happen.

7   Act As If

Before Bruce Springsteen became a rock star he was just a gravelly voiced singer in a bar. Before Robert Kiyosaki became the famous author of *Rich Dad Poor Dad*, he was a copy machine salesman, t-shirt salesman, and had a surfer wallet company that went bankrupt. Theodor Seuss Geisel, better know as Dr. Seuss, worked in advertising before his first book, *And to Think that I Saw It on Mulberry Street*, was rejected as many as thirty times because publishers deemed it "… too different from other juveniles on the market to warrant it's selling."

Imagine that – Dr. Seuss's groundbreaking book was "too different"!

Almost without exception, every superstar, rock star, famous author, revered politician, and business icon, started his or her life as something other than what they became known for. Also nearly without exception, once they found their calling they became that person before it actually happened in the eyes of the public. They began to *act as if* they were a world famous singer, best-selling author, or Grammy-winning actor *before* they became that icon.

What you were or did in the past has little to do with what you can become. We are raised with the expectation to be something (like becoming the same thing your mom or dad does for a career) with your best interests at heart. And yet, that is not who we were designed to be. I was a carpenter and put myself through college and was the first and only one in my family to earn a university degree. I knew that there was something else planned for me other than being a carpenter, so I kept looking until I found it. When you decide who you will be, act as if you are that person already.

You have seen this type of person. She walks into the room and you know that she's "somebody." She walks with purpose and confidence. You can see it in her eyes that she believes in herself and you can tell that she's an inspiration to many. You don't know who she is, but you can tell that she is a person of influence and power.

You have met people like this in a restaurant or at an event. You often find out later that they are the featured speaker, the political candidate, or a Fortune 500 CEO. There is an energy, an aura, and a vibe that successful people have and it is palpable. You are right, they do own something ... they own *themselves*. They may run a business or be a person of power, but most importantly they owns who they were, who they are, and who they will be.

Act as if you are that person *now*. You may not be that person yet (as far as accolades, recognition or other external factors), and that does not matter. Why wait to become successful to be successful? Act as if you are already successful and your success will come quicker and easier. Act as if you are already a superstar and the world will make it happen for you. Act confident and positive about who you are and you will become that person. People want to be around people who are making things happen. People admire someone who is doing something they find appealing. People also love seeing someone on the journey because this inspires them and lets them feel like there is hope and possibility. When others see that you are on a mission they will jump on board and do what they can to help you. A few will go far out of their way to help make you a success because they will feel and believe your conviction.

When you walk with purpose, dress a certain way, carry yourself from a position of strength, and are charismatic, then you actually change your physiology, biology, and psychology. Even when it is just acting you will have real and measurable differences in your body. When you *act as if*, your body doesn't know the difference and it begins to believe the input you give it. In a sense it is a physical affirmation and manifestation.

Do it long enough and it will happen with authenticity.

Let's say you have a big dream you want to make come true. When that happens, you must act as if there is nothing that will stop you. Act as if it has already happened. How do I know that my Run Across America will be successful? Because I see it as already completed. There is no other option, only success. When people ask me about the "what ifs" and doubt talk, I tell them, "I will finish if I have to crawl to New York. I will successed." If you do not exude that confidence that you are going to make it happen, why would anyone buy into your idea and dream? Why would friends, family, or business associates support you if you are wishy-washy? You must act with passion and determination.

Act as if and you will become!

8 Take Action

Sounds simple right? It should be and yet so many fail to take the necessary action to create a life on their terms. Like most people, at times I have been paralyzed with fear. When we don't take action we miss opportunities, we miss going on adventures, meeting amazing people, falling in love, finding new friends and making new business connections. If you do not take action today, when will you? If it does not happen today it never happens.

Today is the day to start a new lifestyle of eating healthy and exercising to get fit.
Today is the day that you start looking for or creating that dream job you have always wanted.
Today is the day that you go back to school or sign up for coaching or training.

If it is not today, you will look back in five years and say, "I should have started back then. If I did I would have already been there." There is only one time to take action. And that is now, today in the moment.

Action has three major distinctions.

1 **First is to take action.**

2 **Second is taking purposeful action.**

3 **Third, it must be massive action.**

These are all very important components. Let's take a closer look.

Have you ever met someone who said, "One day I will open my own business," or "One day I will quit my job and do something I actually enjoy," or "One day I will find time to write a book"? You probably know many people like this. You have probably even said some of these things or something similar. At the end of life people regret all of the things they didn't do, but always wanted to. What are you waiting for?

Do you need a special invitation?

I cordially invite you to take immediate and massive action to make your all your dreams come true.

Consider yourself formally invited.

This is not a joke or even tongue and cheek. Take action! Not just any action, really freakin' massively BIG action! Take immediate action to make your dreams come true. Nobody is going to do it for you. If not today, then when? Tomorrow never comes because there is always something else to do unless you make your dreams a priority above all else. You are amazing and you deserve it. Go make it happen.

When I was a very active real estate investor I would attend the Real Estate Investment Association (REIA) meetings. There were three groups of people. The active investors, brand new attendees seeing what this was all about, and the "wishers." The wishers are people who attend the REIA meetings month after month, year after year, but never buy or partner on a property.

To become an investor you need two things: 1. Some knowledge, and 2. Take action. You don't need *money*, you don't need *experience*, you don't need much of anything. It's easy to do if you can pull the trigger. Wishers never pull the trigger and make an offer. Or they make one or two unreasonable offers and say, "It's impossible."

My best deal was buying a house no money down, no payments, and no attorneys. I was twenty-six years old. It was a handshake deal with an old school fellow who trusted me. I paid his full asking price and then I sold the property a week later to made twenty-five thousand dollars. It was a classic textbook no-money-down flip like I learned in a Carlton sheets home study course. It was a three hundred dollar course. I'd say that was a great return on investment. When someone tells me that something doesn't work and that I am wasting my money on study courses and seminars, I just laugh inside. I made this deal way before I knew much about real estate. Nobody told me I couldn't, I simply took action and asked for what I wanted and needed. You know what? It happened. And that was the very first deal and there have been many since.

At the REIA meetings I met Cathy. She heard that I was an active investor and asked lots of questions. This is good and I was happy to chat about investing. Go to people who have done it before and ask questions. I would see Cathy month after month, year after year, and I would ask her, "Did you make a deal yet?" There was always an excuse. She never made a deal in the time that I knew her and I'll bet that she never did. She couldn't make the jump from wisher to superstar by taking action. Like a shy teenager standing against the wall at the high school dance, Cathy never got to dance.

Take action. When you take action it will build your confidence and you will take more action. Confidence rises in the act of doing. Don't take action and it will get harder and harder to make the first jump. Your confidence will atrophy and expire. It is a spiral that can go up or down. Each day you must take some action towards your goals. Even if you are working at a job (for now) and you are dog-tired, you still must do something that will move you in the direction of your goals TODAY!

9 Take Purposeful Action

Have you ever had a day that starts with ten things on your list and then at the end of the day you have crossed them all off, but you haven't accomplished anything meaningful? You were *busy*, but you weren't *productive*. You did things that may or may not be important and yet you didn't move any closer towards your goals and dreams.

"Don't mistake activity for achievement." – Coach John Wooden

At the speed of life today it is easy to get caught up in the whirlwind of busyness. In two steps you can get rid of the stress and frustration of having too much to do.

1 Eliminate and Minimize

Get rid of anything and everything that is not making your life better or moving you towards your goals. I know what is going in you head, you can rationalize all you want, but it's not going to do you any good. Checking email and Facebook every five minutes is a waste of time. Stop saying "yes" to everything that is asked of you, unless it specifically moves you towards your goals. Saying "yes" to too many things just gets you overwhelmed. Say "yes" to yourself and your family, say "yes" to the things that will bring you closer to your goals, and say "NO" to everything else. It doesn't matter who asks or what they ask for. Leaders know how to say "no" when they need to.

2 Outsource Everything

Are you still cutting your lawn, doing your laundry, food shopping, and cleaning your house? Stop it! Those are minimum-wage activities. Hire those out to someone who wants and needs to do those tasks. The time you save then gets used to work on building your business, your brand, and your dream. You are way too valuable to do everything yourself. Having someone else clean your house and cut your lawn will save you at least three hours a week. They will likely do a better job than you and it will save you money. You don't have to buy and maintain a lawn mower, gets your clothes dirty or get sweaty. Plus it is a great feeling to come home and see your lawn manicured and your house sparkling.

Superstars have laser-like focus on the main target goal. Everything they do moves them towards it or they don't do it. There are no to-do lists, just action lists with the one or two thing that must get done that day. Capture everything that you may have to do and then pick out the one or two most important things that bring you closer to your objective and do those. Do not stop until you complete them. One reason I put together the *Dream Big Act Big* Run Across America in only six months was because I knew that was the shortest time possible and every action had to be focused. Long time-frame goals are unfocused, giving too much room for distraction.

If you are not sure if something will move you towards your goals, try it out and then discard it if it is not helping. I know several people who use networking groups to find new business. They continue to use them to feed their client funnel because it works well for their business and personality. I never had much success with networking groups, so I stopped going unless I'm the feature speaker. I find that being the speaker is a very effective way to find new business and make powerful connections.

Attend different events until you understand which ones are useful and important and which ones are not productive for you. Then drop the time wasters. One of the best investments of time I have made and the best investment I have seen work for so many is Toastmasters. You may or may not make new business, but you will learn to become a better communicator and that will help in every business you are in.

10 Take Massive Action

"Is that possible?" This is the response I get from people when I tell them about my Run Across America. That is the response you want. If people do not doubt what you are doing, you are not doing enough. You can be certain that female racecar driver Danica Patrick hit a lot of resistance and probably a lot of ridicule for wanting to be a professional racer. She is now famous worldwide. She never let others tell her what is not possible for her and now she is the best female racer in history.

You know you are taking massive action when you start making waves and getting resistance from people. It's not that you want to agitate people; it will simply be a matter of course when you are making big things happen. Some people are going to disagree with you. We all like and want different things. So it is natural for some to resist your direction in life. When that happens you know you are on the right track. I know that I am doing the right thing *for me* when I get resistance from people who are not my target market. I also know I am doing the right thing *for me* when I am inspiring people who are in my market.

Massive action is quitting your stable and solid job as a teacher to follow your passion as an amateur female bodybuilder and professional fitness guru, like my friend Dawn Robertson. Massive action is when Sylvester Stallone refused to take a job to pay the bills and continued to pursue his love for acting and script writing, costing him everything before he broke through.

The story of Sylvester Stallone is as legendary as the movie *Rocky*. When Stallone was starting out as an actor, the only thing he had was a big dream. At that time he had only acted in a couple of really small parts, one of which he was thug who got beat up.

One night Stallone's watching the boxing match between Muhammad Ali and Chuck Wepner. The challenger, Wepner, refuses to give up. Ali keeps dancing around in his charismatic style and he keeps pounding Wepner. But he won't go down. The challenger gets hit over and over, round after round. Wepner lasts the whole fight, fifteen rounds of bloody, punishing boxing.

As Stallone is watching this fight he is inspired by Wepner's refusal to give up. Stallone cannot believe the punishment that this guy has taken and he keeps coming back for more. Stallone is struck by the parallel to his life and thinks, "This is *my* life. This is what life is about, you get hit and you must keep getting up."

Once the fight ends Stallone gets a pad and pen and writes the movie script to *Rocky*. He doesn't stop for more than thirty hours. He loves the script and he goes out to try to sell it. Nobody will buy it. They say its predictable, its corny, and nobody is going to want to see a movie about a boxer. Stallone is unfazed by his hundreds of rejections. He continues to go out over and over to the producers to sell his script. Meanwhile he's dead broke. As the story goes, in a moment of desperation he sells his wife's jewelry. Reminiscing on the course of his life, Stallone said, "There is one thing you should never do!" referring to hocking her jewelry.

Stallone goes to every producer in New York City over and over and over, as many as one thousand five hundred rejections. There aren't nearly that many producers in all of New York. Stallone goes to the same producers eight, nine, and ten times before he finally he gets two producers to bite. They call him into their office and offer him a reported one-hundred-twenty-five thousand dollars.

Stallone thanks them, but tells them that he must star in the movie. The producers laugh at him, saying, "You're a writer, not an actor." Stallone insists that he has to act in it. The producers say, "No way." Stallone is still broke at this time, and he takes the script and walks away. He walks because he knows his outcome. He saw his vision and wouldn't accept anything less than making his dream come true. Imagine being offered over one hundred thousand dollars back in 1975 when you don't have twenty-five dollars in your pocket, and you walk away.

A few weeks later the producers call him back up and offer him double the money *not* to act in the film! Stallone says that the only way he will sell the movie is if he can star in it, and he walks away again. A few weeks later the producers call him up. They will let him star in the movie, but Stallone has to take the risk too. They pay him only eighteen thousand dollars and points in the film. Stallone agrees. *Rocky* cost just over one million to make and grossed over $225 million dollars.

The legend of the making of *Rocky* and Stallone's decision to walk away unless he played the main role is the classic story of the underdog who finally makes it. Like all legends the story is probably embellished, but it is truly a story of what you must do to make your dreams a reality. Stallone could have gotten a job when he was trying to sell *Rocky*, but he didn't because he knew that he would lose his drive and be seduced into complacency. The same complacency that woos millions of talented and unknown superstars into accepting so much less than what they are capable of.

For ten years of my life I had fallen for complacency because it seemed so easy. A nice house and car living in the suburbs making a comfortable income. It seems so picturesque. Taking what seems like the easy road, what seems like it is the American dream, eventually turns out to be a nightmare. One day you will wake up as I did and ask, "Is this all there is?" Like many people approaching midlife, I started asking, "What is my purpose in life? What will I be remembered for?" Sometimes to get what you want you have to be willing to give up the good to get the great.

Superstar Strategies

Here is the list of the Strategies of a Superstar for review. Dog-ear the page, write these on your wall, keep them in your wallet, or post them on your car's sun-visor. Somewhere you will see it everyday.

Strategies of a Superstar

1	Go Big!	6	Be Relentless
2	Be Infectious With Enthusiasm	7	Act As If
3	Boldness is Rewarded	8	Take Action
4	Be Amazing	9	Take Purposeful Action
5	Be Outrageous	10	Take Massive Action

Harness Your X-Factor

Think of someone you met whom you instantly liked. You may have even said to a friend, "I can't put my finger on it, but there is something really special about her. She's got *IT!*" You don't know what it is, but you are drawn to that person. It is that amazing *thing* that makes that person so extraordinary and it only takes a few seconds for you to sense it.

That's her X-Factor. It is the indescribable *thing* that makes someone stand out and above others. When someone has a powerful X-Factor, everyone else knows it because they can see it, feel it, hear it, and sense it. It is an energy that is palpable.

All great actors have an extraordinary X-Factor. Examples are Clark Gable, Marilyn Monroe, Sean Connery, Angelina Jolie, and Morgan Freeman. Revolutionaries also have an intense X-Factor such as GE CEO Jack Welch, Apple CEO Steve Jobs, and Presidents John F. Kennedy, Bill Clinton, and Barack Obama.

We all have an X-Factor. Most people suppress it or deny it. Some aren't aware of it. Few understand it. Leaders harness it and champions live it. Your X-Factor may be your most important asset. If you ignore it or deny it, you are severely limiting what you will do and where you will go in life. Like a fingerprint, this is the thing that makes you unique.

Your X-factor is your BAM! That indescribable thing that makes you unique and spectacular. It's your vital quality that cannot be defined with precision. To say that Marilyn Monroe had sex appeal is an understatement. She was so much more. Marilyn had a unique code of mystery, vitality, femininity, sensuality, and strength. I say "code" because that is what it is. Like a code that delivers a secret message.

The X factor can be a massive amount of www.wisegeek.com/what-is-charisma.htm charisma such as Sir Richard Branson or odd charisma like Jim Carrey. It can be confidence and an air of ambition. It can also be a quite sense of power and leadership. X-Factor is most often though of as some who is exuberant and charismatic, but it can also be quite and calm like Mahatma Gandhi and the Dali Lama.

The X-Factor is what defines a superstar. There are many amazing dancers who will dazzle you with their techniques and abilities. The ones that stand out are the ones who "just have it." They have a palpable personality or special sense of artistry in adding motion to the music. While technically similar to the other dancers, the superstar evokes emotion in her audience because she adds her essence to the dance.

What is it about you that makes you unique and special? Is it your charisma, your charm, your sex appeal, athletic ability, intelligence, quirkiness, humor, or your ability to make people feel special? There is something amazing about you and it is your X-Factor. Let that extraordinary *thing* about you shine. Foster and nourish it to grow and stand out. It's what makes you attractive to others. Some of what makes you extraordinary is innate. Most of what makes you extraordinary needs to be mastered. Do whatever it takes to cultivate your X-Factor. Take lessons, get coaching, and practice. Did you know that Coach Vince Lombardi would practice his game face, mean face, and his other expressions in the mirror? He polished his craft down to the detail of his expressions. Lombardi understood the importance of perfecting your brand and persona.

BECOMING THE SUPERSTAR

You totally rock! I mean it! You are totally amazing. If you read to the last chapter in *Dream Big Act Big*, then you are committed to becoming extraordinary. You are in the top one percent of everyone in the world in your commitment to personal empowerment. From my heart, I congratulate you.

Because you are so amazing, I have a special gift for you. Go to www. DreamBigActBig.com/bookbonus and download your free bonus training. This is my gift to you for being so devoted to making an amazing life. Because you took action and because you followed through, I want to help you continue to grow and achieve and Breakthrough to Unleash The Superstar Within.

Before you go, I have one last essential thought for you. I wish I could wave a magic wand over your head and make all your dreams come true in an instant. I can't. Nobody can. However, all of your dreams can come true and you can create an amazing life with the lessons and strategies in the pages of this book. It's all right here. These are the lessons and strategies that made me one of the best in the world and they can do it for you as well.

It only works if you are committed to creating a life of adventure. It only works if you are dedicated to making it happen. In the words of the great Sir Winston Churchill, "Never give in! Never, never, never!" You must always be relentless in your pursuit of improving and achieving in career, relationships, love, family, and adventure. Life is about the experience. The more you take action, the more you will see, do, have and be. Keep moving forward even when it feels like you are not making progress. You are always making progress. Sometimes you plateau and then one day, BAM, you break through with a leap forward. The plateau, the dip, the hard part, the challenges are all there to self-eliminate those who are not serious about becoming a superstar and creating an extraordinary life.

You are different. You are unique. You are special. You have what it takes to make it big. You have the ability to achieve your dreams. You are here on this blue globe for a reason. That reason is to make a difference in this world. Will you improve other's lives, help the environment, save wildlife, create a revolutionary product, discover a cure, support an amazing cause, or some other fantastic thing? You will do something amazing because you can and because you are designed to do something amazing.

And most importantly, you are taking action!

You have probably had a challenging past. It is time for you to rise above your past and step boldly into your future. It is time to commit to your adventure. In the past you may have been limited by old beliefs. Those beliefs no longer serve you and you can now let those go and adopt the new beliefs that will serve you better. You may have had others tell you what is possible for you and what is not. You now understand that anything is possible and other's words will no longer stop you. The only words that matter are the words you tell and say to yourself. When you are in a moment of doubt yell this out loud and proclaim your worth,

"I am a Superstar!
No one will deny me and nobody will define me!
I am the only one who will decide who I am!
I am the only who will decide who I will become!
My belief in who I am will power my mind!
My actions will revolutionize my world!
because I am a Champion!
I am a Superstar!"

You are a champion. You are a superstar. Keep moving forward. Keep improving. Keep making one-degree changes and live a life of Kaizen. Follow the mantra of actor Will Smith, "Nobody will expect more from me than I expect of myself." Live a life of excellence even when nobody is watching. Practice, study, and hone your skills before anyone has ever heard of you. Do it for yourself. Believe in yourself. And become the person you were designed to be.

EPILOGUE

I am honored to have spent this time with you. We are kindred spirits and the universe has brought us together for a reason. Please email me your comments to info@dreambigactbig.com and become a fan and a friend on Facebook.

My Run Across America and my foundation will continue to put books in the hands of those young adults who have little more than the drive to succeed. The magical part is that the drive is all you need. Everything else can be learned. The foundation will also be giving scholarships, training programs and so much more to those who embrace the belief that "If it is to be, it is up to me." Please help us make the world a better place by sponsoring a mile. If you are interested in applying to receive a book, training or scholarship, please go to www.DreamBigActBig.com.

I am writing my next book already. It is all about you. The book will be about your success stories. I will be collecting and interviewing people as I run across America and on the yearlong speaking tour afterwards. Please share your story of overcoming adversity, rising above your past, and the amazing things you have achieved. This next book will be a compilation of over one hundred short stories of success and growth.

And finally a few superstar thoughts as a bonus.

With Gratitude Comes More Gifts

We are defined by the meaning we give to things in our life. This is why someone who goes through inconceivably horrible events can go on to achieve so much, help so many others and make a huge difference in this world. Those who overcome horrific challenges in life view those challenges as the foundation that has made them strong and resilient.

Superstars say, "It was the challenges in my life that have brought to where I am today. If it were not for those challenges, I would not understand the world as I do and would not be as strong as I am. I would not have achieved what I did." People who have gone through the most horrific of experiences also understand that they have chosen the meaning if their past. They chose for it to give them strength. They are not the victims, they ARE the VICTORS!

Focus on what is great in your life and you will find more greatness in your life and more will be able to enter. Did you know that people want to give you money and gifts? All your life they have tried. If you do not readily and graciously accept their gifts then you will be unable to see the gifts when they come to you in the future.

My grandmother would never accept a gift from anyone. Even at Christmas time she would find a way to give you the gift back, return it for you, or give you an equivalent amount of money. She was a giver and it was always at her expense. Financially, emotionally and psychologically.

On the other hand, my uncle was a taker. He took from everyone he could. If it wasn't nailed down, it somehow became his. If it were the property of a family member he would figure out a way to guilt you into giving it to him, or swindle it from you. He took, took, and took. Always at someone else's expense.

My grandfather understood the balance of giving and receiving. After my grandmother would tell me that it is impolite to take gifts from others, my grandfather would come over and have a chat with me. He told me this many times though my younger years. He would say, "It is polite to refuse a gift once, but if it is offered twice or insisted upon you, graciously say 'thank you.' If you refuse the gift you will offend the giver. God makes things happen for a reason."

Only those who can graciously and genuinely accept gifts can continue to get more gifts. And in return for being so blessed they also give freely to others. We are all connected. It is our privilege to be able to receive and give to pay it forward. They world can only get better when we work together and share with others. You never know how you are going to touch the life of another. Like throwing pebbles in a pond, the ripple effects go far beyond the initial splash.

Tell us your story

The process of sharing is also the process of learning, healing, and teaching. I have found incredible clarity and cleansing in sharing my stories. What once imprisoned me, now empowers me because I have found the lesson in the event and gave that gift to others. Please share your story of overcoming adversity, rising above your past, and the amazing things you have achieved. If your story is chosen, it will be used in my next book. info@DreamBigActBig.com

Did you love Dream Big Act Big?

Each time that I find a great book, I want to share it. Sometimes I buy additional copies and pass them along to special people in my life. It bothers me that I buy several copies and have to pay full price for each one. So I am breaking the rules. Order directly from www.DreamBigActBig.com and use special discount code *PayItForward* and save 30% when you buy 5 or more copies.

Success Coaching

The best athletes in the world and the best business professionals all have one thing in common. They have the best coaching. Success Coaching will be tailored to your needs and goals. The objective is simple – to create a life by your design.

For details go to www.DreamBigActBig.com/Coaching

Home Learning Products

Learn from the comfort of your home and during "NET Time" like driving in your car. Home study courses are a great way to learn new strategies and also reinforce strategies you already learned. As it is said, "Repetition is the mother of all skill." Go to www.DreamBigActBig.com/products

Speaking Engagements

Croix Sather is a dynamic award-winning speaker. His presentations are a combination of edge-of-your-seat stories, real life experiences, and world-class strategies to bring your company or group to Superstar levels. Some teach strategies, Croix lives them and then programs you for success.

To have Croix motivate, inspire and program your group for success email info@DreamBigActBig.com

Guest Appearances

To have Croix Sather at your event, promotion and for sponsorship email media@DreamBigActBig.com

Non-Profit Events

Croix Sather strongly believes in giving back to the betterment of this small world that we inhabit and the people who share it. Croix supports local, national and international charities. Dream Big Act Big books are available in gratitude to organizations that serve at risk adults. Croix gives many in-kind presentations each year to organizations that support and help others. Learn more at www.DreamBigActBig.com and www.CroixSather.com or email info@DreamBigActBig.com

ABOUT THE AUTHOR

Some people teach strategies to create an extraordinary life and others live it. Croix is proving what he teaches with a 3,000 mile Run Across America.

Sounds exciting, right? Not yet. Each day he is also speaking to at-risk young adults. That's a speech and an Ultra-marathon (30 miles) run each day for 100 consecutive days.

Life Changes in a Moment ...

There's no medical reason why Croix is alive. At age fourteen his life would change forever. The speeding drunk driver never saw the young boy riding home on his bicycle when her car hit Croix head-on, crushing his bike and launching him 50 feet before he crashed into the ground. With his body mangled, he was rushed to the trauma center.

The Neurosurgeon said to his parents, "If he survives the night, he will be a vegetable for the rest of his life." The doctor's valiant efforts pulled Croix through. He spent almost four days in a coma, two weeks in the hospital, and more than a year in physical rehabilitation. Debilitating headaches from his fractured skull lasted for years. And memory challenges persisted for two decades.

After the brutal car crash, life was different. He lost his drive and went into a downward spiral. He used the accident as "the excuse" for his failures leading him down a misguided "indiscretions." As a young adult he would become "successful", but he kept self-sabotaging his achievements.

Fate once again intervened ...

Croix was introduced to the world of personal empowerment. It was in this environment that he found others like himself that were restless and bored ... wanting so much more out of life. These people "got it" and were kindred souls. Croix immersed himself in training with the top experts around the world in the areas of communication, success psychology, subconscious reprogramming, NLP, hypnotherapy, and more.

Croix learned to breakthrough and become a superstar. He now teaches those empowering strategies in this book and his seminars. We all have seeds of greatness. Learn how to make your seeds of greatness flourish and create an amazing life beyond measure.

Run Across America

Croix is now sharing the lessons in this book during his Run Across America Inspirational Tour. Croix will be running an ultra-marathon (30 miles) a day, plus a keynote seminar for 100 consecutive days. His keynote speeches to at-risk young adults are free.

100,000 books give-a-way

Croix knows that his life would have been different if he had a success coach earlier in life. He wishes that he had someone that showed him the strategies, gave him the tools, and taught him the programming to be extraordinary. Without the lessons he learned from his experiences, his mentors, and his dedication to self-empowerment, his life would still be a mess. Now Croix is committed to sharing these strategies with as many people as possible. This is why Croix is committed to donating 100,000 *Dream Big Act Big* books to at-risk adults and organizations that help others.